YOUR GUIDE
TO THE
APOCALYPSE

YOUR GUIDE TO THE APOCALYPSE

WHAT YOU SHOULD KNOW BEFORE THE WORLD COMES TO AN END

MATT HAGEE

WATERBROOK

Your Guide to the Apocalypse

All Scripture quotations, unless otherwise indicated, are taken from the New King James Version®. Copyright © 1982 by Thomas Nelson Inc. Used by permission. All rights reserved. Scripture quotations marked (KJV) are taken from the King James Version. Scriptures quotations marked (NIV) are taken from the Holy Bible, New International Version®, NIV®. Copyright © 1973, 1978, 1984 by Biblica Inc.® Used by permission. All rights reserved worldwide.

Italics in Scripture quotations reflect the author's added emphasis.

Trade Paperback ISBN 978-1-60142-992-6
eBook ISBN 978-1-60142-993-3

Copyright © 2017 by Matthew Hagee

Cover design by Mark D. Ford

Published in the United States by WaterBrook, an imprint of the Crown Publishing Group, a division of Penguin Random House LLC, New York.

WATERBROOK® and its deer colophon are registered trademarks of Penguin Random House LLC.

Library of Congress Cataloging-in-Publication Data
Names: Hagee, Matthew, author.
Title: Your guide to the Apocalypse : what you should know before the world comes to an end
  / Matthew Hagee.
Description: First Edition. | Colorado Springs, Colorado : WaterBrook, 2017. | Includes
  bibliographical references. |
Identifiers: LCCN 2017011124 (print) | LCCN 2017026718 (ebook) | ISBN 9781601429933
  (electronic) | ISBN 9781601429926 (pbk.)
Subjects: LCSH: End of the world.
Classification: LCC BT877 (ebook) | LCC BT877 .H34 2017 (print) | DDC 236/.9—dc23
LC record available at https://lccn.loc.gov/2017011124

Printed in the United States of America
2017

10 9 8 7 6 5 4 3

SPECIAL SALES
Most WaterBrook books are available at special quantity discounts when purchased in bulk by corporations, organizations, and special-interest groups. Custom imprinting or excerpting can also be done to fit special needs. For information, please e-mail specialmarketscms@ penguinrandomhouse.com or call 1-800-603-7051.

To my grandparents: Rev. William Bythel Hagee
and Mrs. Vada Swick Hagee

———

Your love for God and His Word is the soil that our
family tree is planted in. From the roots of your lives,
your descendants have branched out to touch the nations
of the world with the gospel of Jesus Christ. For all that
you did that remained unseen—for the sacrifices you
made, the legacy you left, and those you won to
Christ—today I rise up and call you blessed. This work
is dedicated in honor of all that you both meant to me.

Praise for
Your Guide to the Apocalypse

"As we watch news headlines and current events unfold, it's hard not to think about how they might coincide with biblical prophecies. If you've ever wondered what the Bible says about end times and what we're experiencing in our world today, then *Your Guide to the Apocalypse* by my friend Matt Hagee is the book for you! Using Scripture, he reveals the answers that will give you a greater understanding of God's plan for all humanity as well as His purpose for your life."

—ROBERT MORRIS, founding senior pastor of Gateway
Church, Dallas/Fort Worth, Texas, and best-selling author
of *The Blessed Life* and *The God I Never Knew*

"Pastor Matt Hagee has done it again! *Your Guide to the Apocalypse* faces the hard biblical truth of how Christians need to respond to the world. The Bible is specific about how the end times will look, and Pastor Matt provides a clear road map for the church and followers of Christ. I am thankful for this book, as it is one of a kind."

—PASTOR MATTHEW BARNETT, co-founder of The Dream
Center and *New York Times* best-selling author of *The
Cause Within You*

"In a world where feelings and opinions are held in higher esteem than truth, it is easy to get lost in the false prophecies and confusion. Pastor Matt Hagee calls attention to the one reliable truth—God's Word—and provides an easy-to-follow, factual guide to help us navigate these tumultuous days."

—DAVID BARTON, founder of WallBuilders

"Pastor Matt Hagee explains how developments in governments, technology, and world events are connected to and fulfilling biblical prophecy."

—JENTEZEN FRANKLIN, senior pastor of Free Chapel and *New York Times* best-selling author

CONTENTS

The Christian Church and the Apocalypse

The Rapture and the Tribulation to Come

FOREWORD

The world is fascinated with the future of planet Earth. The rich and powerful are digging underground cities, looking over their shoulders at the possibility of a nuclear mushroom cloud on the horizon. Average citizens are stocking up on dehydrated foods, water supplies, and weapons for the world tomorrow.

Will Russia once again become the mighty USSR? Will Iran attack Israel with new superweapons made possible by America's $150 billion gift? Will there be a major terrorist attack on America?

Will Israel be ready for the coming war in the Middle East? Will North Korea launch an intercontinental ballistic missile targeted for New York City? Will the global financial markets crash, leaving the world swimming in absolute poverty?

Matthew Hagee has taken the prophetic road map provided by Daniel, Jesus of Nazareth, and John the Revelator to show us the world tomorrow. *Your Guide to the Apocalypse* is a page-turner that fully explains how the world as we know it will end!

—John Hagee
Author of *Four Blood Moons* and *Jerusalem Countdown*

THE UNVEILING OF A MYSTERY

Behold, I tell you a mystery.

—1 Corinthians 15:51

magine you are at a trade show and the latest designs in your industry are on display all over the showroom floor. As usual at these events, the executives, engineers, and salespeople from each company have done all they can to distinguish for the buyers why their new design, new product, or latest innovation should be preferred over the competition's. But there's something different at this trade show.

In the center of the showroom is a massive curtain hung in a circle, stretching from ceiling to floor, so that it hides one of the offerings. The huge veil is too thick to see through, and guards are stationed all around it to prevent anyone from lifting it up and sneaking a peek at what awaits on the other side. The room is buzzing about this display. Everyone is curious about the revelation that is to come. They are all speculating without any real clue, because none of them has been on the other side.

Some guess that whatever is hiding behind the curtain is nothing impressive, and they attempt to convince others of their view.

They go so far as to accuse anyone who does not agree with them of being ignorant and closed-minded. While they have no understanding of what's behind the curtain, they are committed to claiming it's a hoax.

Others carry on about how awesome this mystery must be. They imagine what is about to be unveiled. They hypothesize about how you can gain access to the product and who you need to know to get in. They are better meaning than the skeptics, but at the same time, they do not possess any more knowledge than the first group. They have not been on the other side of the veil, but at least they are willing to believe that something is really there.

Suddenly, while the crowd presses in closer to the mysterious curtain, someone touches your shoulder and motions for you to follow him. Cutting a path through the crowd, he takes you to the other side. A guard steps aside to let the two of you pass. Then your guide leads you to the curtain, separates it where the edges meet, and pulls back one side to reveal to you what everyone else is wondering about. There it is!

This, in effect, is what the Bible does for those who study biblical prophecy. It pulls back the curtain, revealing what others are merely speculating about and struggling with regarding what will happen when the world as we know it comes to an end. The word *apocalypse* comes from the Greek language and refers to "an unveiling." Just as in our example about someone unveiling the hidden trade-show display to you, so Scripture unveils the mystery of the end times.

And isn't the fate of the world something you'd like to know about?

Even more important, don't you think you ought to understand what you need to do to be ready for what is to come?

THE ABSOLUTE TRUTH

We live in a world that offers several options displayed on the show floor about how we should live. More so than at any other time in history, whatever we choose to do or not do, be or not be, identify with or detest, anything goes! The issue that some choose to ignore and others face in their own way is this large, heavy curtain that is in front of all of us. Call it the end times, the apocalypse, the last days, or anything else you please—it's there. All of history has led up to this moment, and the entire world and heaven above are awaiting its unveiling.

What is crucial is choosing the correct source of information about what lies ahead. We need a reliable guide, like the man in my story who escorted you to the curtain and pulled it aside. The one and only reliable guide is the Holy Scriptures.

In a world where people take for granted that there are no absolutes, the Bible is in reality the absolute truth. This book I have written will demonstrate the Bible's prophetic accuracy when describing the events that would occur in world history long before they ever happened. Therefore, the Bible is not just in the ballpark; it is absolutely on target. We can trust it when it comes to deciding what major world events will happen next.

Several parts of the Bible refer to the end times. Let's consider a few of the passages in the Bible that let us know what truths God is revealing:

- The disciples received an unveiling when they asked Christ, "Tell us, when will these things be? And what will be the sign of Your coming, and of the end of the age?" (Matthew 24:3). Christ went on to speak about the events that would be happening to the Jewish people and the nation of Israel from the first century until what is known as the Great Tribulation.

- The apostle Paul received an unveiling that he shared in his writings to the church of Corinth: "Behold, I tell you a mystery: We shall not all sleep, but we shall all be changed—in a moment, in the twinkling of an eye, at the last trumpet. For the trumpet will sound, and the dead will be raised incorruptible, and we shall be changed" (1 Corinthians 15:51–52). He mentioned the same revelation to the church in Thessalonica, to whom he wrote, "We who are alive and remain shall be caught up together . . . in the clouds to meet the Lord in the air" (1 Thessalonians 4:17). This word picture is describing what is known as the Rapture, when Jesus returns to claim His followers and remove them from the earth before a time of judgment.

- The apostle John, on the isle of Patmos, experienced an unveiling that he recorded in the first chapter of the book of Revelation: "I was in the Spirit on the Lord's Day, and I heard behind me a loud voice" (verse 10). That voice was the voice of the Alpha and Omega—Jesus Christ—who presented to John an unveiling of what must take place.

By reading and studying such texts, we seize the opportunity to understand what others can only wonder about. What an amazing privilege it is to have this foresight!

Right now, the leading governments of the world are engaged in a massive power struggle. It involves military strength and strategy, economic influence, and diplomatic policy. Coercion, sanctions, and plain old schoolyard bullying are going on. Why? Because they all desperately want to be the first to know who is going to dominate the world as the next global superpower. China, Russia, Iran, Europe, and the United States are speculating about a matter that was settled long ago.

If you take the time to study Bible prophecy, then you know that the curtain has already been pulled back. You have been given a clear glimpse of what is now only slowly being leaked by the major news outlets of our day.

Why is Russia in the Middle East? Why is the United States struggling to recover its once-dominant position in the world? Why is Iran chanting, "Death to America" and "Death to Israel"? And why is the U.S. State Department giving the Iranians billions of dollars to create nuclear weapons and fund terrorism? Why, at times like these, are people more concerned about the Wi-Fi password at their local coffee shop than they are about the rise of ISIS and the failure of the world's response to radical Islamic jihad?

Why is all of this going on in the world? Some say it's random. Others want to blame failed policies, political trends, or cultural shifts. But the absolute truth is that the Word of God spelled out these details, letter by letter and line for line, centuries before we found them trending on Twitter.

When there is no natural answer to be found, then the best place to search is in the supernatural resource of Scripture, and the facts lie in the unveiling of what has become known as the apocalypse.

UNVEILED

In the pages that follow, it is my intention to introduce you to truth. There are certainly more in-depth studies that fully explain every detail and aspect of the prophetic, historical, and cultural indicators surrounding the end times and the apocalypse. My purpose is to connect some major concepts at the surface, not take you all the way through the entirety of its content in one work. I've also recorded some of my teaching on video, which you can find at Jhm.org/apocalypse, to give you further insight into how prophecy ties to current events.

I believe the easiest way to grasp the complex is to keep it simple, and the simple truth is that we are the generation that will see the return of Jesus Christ. To prove it, I will present three major prophetic and historical arenas as the focus of this book. These arenas were 98 percent prophecy and 2 percent historical fact when first written on scrolls, but now, centuries later, they are reversed—98 percent are history and the 2 percent left is the moment that generations have been waiting for.

The three unveilings that we will consider are the following:

First, we will look at the writings of Daniel when he gave the interpretation to King Nebuchadnezzar's dream, and then later to a vision he received from the Lord. Both give an exact account of the powers that would rule the world, from the days of Babylon to the global struggle of nations at the United Nations today. Daniel didn't miss one detail, and the portion of his vision that hasn't come to pass describes a King and a kingdom for which there will be no end.

Then there is the answer that Jesus Christ gave to His disciples before His arrest and crucifixion. They asked Him, "What will be the sign of Your coming?" (Matthew 24:3). His answer gave an exact description of what would happen to the Jewish people and the nation of Israel from AD 70, when Titus conquered Jerusalem, until we see "the Son of Man coming on the clouds of heaven with power and great glory" (Matthew 24:30). Christ was so precise that we can track the events of history for the last two thousand years and see how every word has come to pass thus far. We can also see how the events that have not yet come to pass are about to happen.

The final unveiling comes from the first chapters of the book of Revelation. John had a dialogue with the resurrected Jesus Christ, who had specific messages for the seven churches of Asia. These letters were not only personal and written for their generation, but they are also prophetic, addressing what the church will be like throughout history until the return of Christ to the earth.

Matthew 18:16 states, "By the mouth of two or three witnesses every word may be established." We have the prophet Daniel, Jesus Christ in Matthew 24, and John the Revelator all confirming what will happen in the world until the end of time. All these witnesses testify to this conclusion: Christ is coming back and it will be sooner than many may think.

A CAUSE FOR HOPE

There are people in every group, be it religious, political, financial, or just plain secular, whose personal desires don't line up with what God has set in motion. They do all they can to claim that prophecies have been misunderstood, that the Bible is too complex to understand, and that people who preach about the terminal generation and the return of Christ are marketing fear and a doomsday gospel.

I assure you, nothing could be further from the truth. The Bible is a book of hope. The return of Christ is a promise of deliverance that is to come. What you are about to read is intended to help you understand that the same One who began the world with a word has told us how He plans to take care of those who believe in Him and have received

His Son, until the last second this world turns and the first moment when eternity begins.

I said I like to keep it simple. God did not go through the trouble of revealing His plan in prophecy so that we could argue about the mailing address of the Antichrist, or so that pre-, mid-, post-tribbers (if you're not familiar with those terms, that's okay) could blog about why the others are a bunch of heretics. He didn't preserve the prophetic Scriptures so that we could combine the milk and meat of the Word with the hocus-pocus of the world in trying to determine the exact date and time when the clouds will split and we will see Jesus face-to-face.

He gave us this message so that we would have a source of confidence that will build our faith in a world that does all it can to destroy it. He did it so that we can be light in an hour of darkness and so that we will do all we possibly can to make sure that as many people as we know are ready to meet the Lord when the time comes. He did it so we will be assured that His promise is true: "I go to prepare a place for you. And if I go and prepare a place for you, I will come again and receive you to Myself" (John 14:2–3). It's just that simple.

This is an exciting time to be alive, and it's not by accident that you are on this stage at this exact moment. As the curtain is pulled back on the final scenes, rejoice! God is in control and everything is going to be all right.

Let Us Pray

In my twenty years of pulpit ministry, I have always included in the introduction of my topic a prayer. I believe wholeheartedly that prayer works. I would be remiss if I didn't offer you as a reader, and myself as the author of this work, the opportunity to agree in prayer that our eyes shall be opened to see and our ears to hear what the Word of God has to say in these final moments of the last days. So with that, I offer this prayer:

Heavenly Father, You are the Creator of heaven and earth, and You have been almighty from the beginning of time and to its end. Allow Your Spirit to lead us and guide us as we open the lamp and light of Your truth, walking along this straight and narrow path that leads to the promise of Your return and our ultimate salvation. May these pages bring hope to the readers and confidence to every heart that receives them. May our understanding of Your plan for our lives grow as we accept Your will as You have made it known in Your Word, and may we each accept our responsibility in not only watching and waiting but also working with all of our heart, soul, mind, and strength to share Your love with others so that they may be ready for Your imminent return and may rejoice in Your salvation.

In the name of Christ our Savior, we pray. Amen.

A TROUBLING DREAM OF THE FUTURE

"I am the Alpha and the Omega, the Beginning and the End," says the
Lord, "who is and who was and who is to come, the Almighty."

—Revelation 1:8

Curiously enough, the first person to get a glimpse of the end times was not a Jewish prophet but an idol-worshipping king. His name was Nebuchadnezzar. From 586 to 539 BC, he ruled over the Babylonian Empire, which at the time included the conquered land of Judah (what was left of the old nation of Israel) within its borders.

One night in his bedroom, King Nebuchadnezzar was troubled by a dream, and true to his temperamental nature, if it bothered him, then he was going to make sure it bothered everyone else. Here was the problem: not only did he have a dream and not know what it meant, but also he couldn't remember the contents of the dream and so he wasn't able to share them with any of the fortune-tellers and sorcerers upon whom he depended for supernatural service.

As motivation, he told all of the stargazers, wise men, and warlocks in Babylon that if they didn't tell him what he had dreamed and give him an accurate interpretation of it, he would have them cut into pieces and would burn down their houses. Just in case they thought he was kidding, he made his point clear by adding, "You see that my decision is firm" (Daniel 2:8). Talk about a nasty attitude and a hostile work environment!

When the wise men of Babylon told the king it was impossible, Nebuchadnezzar kept his promise and ordered them to be killed. But Daniel, a political prisoner from Judah, heard what was happening and asked the king to allow him a little more time to inquire of the Lord, the God of Israel, so he could give the king the answers he sought.

Daniel gathered his friends and began to pray, seeking God's mercy, and He answered their prayers, just as He will graciously respond whenever we ask anything of Him. Then when Daniel received the answer, he proclaimed these words:

> Blessed be the name of God forever and ever,
> For wisdom and might are His.
> And He changes the times and the seasons;
> He removes kings and raises up kings;
> He gives wisdom to the wise
> And knowledge to those who have understanding.
> He reveals deep and secret things;
> He knows what is in the darkness,
> And light dwells with Him. (Daniel 2:20–22)

Note especially how Daniel said, "He changes the times and the seasons; He removes kings and raises up kings." Based on this one statement, we can conclude that all that happens in the world, as it changes around us, is measured in the full scope of what God wants to accomplish on earth. He, in essence, is not adjusting to us; we are the ones who are to be mindful of Him.

Every kingdom that has ever been established; every ruler who has ever sat on a throne; every dictator who has ever abused his power over others; every kingdom, republic, or society of any kind—all of them were allowed by God and used to fulfill His purpose, which He set in motion before time began. That is why the greeting John received in the book of Revelation states, "I am the Alpha and the Omega, the Beginning and the End" (Revelation 1:8).

Daniel received an unveiling of God's activity in history. He was given the dream the king had in his bedchamber, and Daniel returned to the palace of this king who would just as soon kill him as hear him speak. He took a deep breath of confidence and said, "You, O king, were watching; and behold, a great image!" (Daniel 2:31).

As I imagine the scene, Nebuchadnezzar sat up straight and stared with eyes of cold steel at the bony prophet standing before him.

Daniel continued. "This great image, whose splendor was excellent, stood before you; and its form was awesome."

The king listened still closer.

Daniel elaborated. "This image's head was of fine gold, its chest and arms of silver, its belly and thighs of bronze, its legs of iron, its feet partly of iron and partly of clay" (verses 32–33).

Nebuchadnezzar softened his scowl. "Yes, yes!" he perhaps declared. "That's what I dreamed. Tell me what it means."

Daniel went on to do just that. And what he told the king reveals for us a progression of kingdoms that reaches to the present day. We are witnessing the march of time leading up to our generation and telling us that we stand on the brink of the final revelation of God's plan for history.

NEBUCHADNEZZAR'S STATUE

Daniel described to the king in detail how each section of the statue represented a different kingdom that would rule the world. Not only does the statue from top to bottom symbolize the order of the kingdoms, but also, after closer analysis, we see that it reflects the characteristics of each kingdom within its historical period.

The Head of the Statue

The head made of gold was Nebuchadnezzar and his Babylonian Empire. Daniel said, "You, O king, are a king of kings" (Daniel 2:37). Notice he did not say "*the* King of kings." Nebuchadnezzar wasn't the Lord. But he was a mighty ruler who had lesser rulers underneath his authority.

Nebuchadnezzar and Babylon were the first of the kingdoms to rule the world. While there had been other rulers who ruled over their own land, Nebuchadnezzar was the first to make other nations subject to him.

The Chest and Arms

The chest and arms of silver came next. This section of the figure symbolized the Medo-Persian kingdom (539–332 BC), which replaced the Babylonian Empire.

Daniel actually lived to see this change of regimes.

When Nebuchadnezzar's grandson Belshazzar was on the throne, Daniel told the current ruler he was about to be replaced: "Your kingdom has been divided, and given to the Medes and Persians" (Daniel 5:28). What happened? "That very night Belshazzar, king of the Chaldeans, was slain. And Darius the Mede received the kingdom" (verses 30–31).

Much earlier, Daniel had declared to Nebuchadnezzar that it was God in heaven who knew the times, changed the seasons, and established kings. Now that very thing happened. The hand of God wrote on the wall that it wasn't the Babylonians, nor the Medes and Persians, who made the ultimate decision about when power and control would change. That authority came directly from the God who created heaven and earth. Personally, I take great comfort in knowing that someone who loves and cares for me so much is in total control.

But history's progress was far from over.

The Belly and Thighs

The next section of the statue, which was the belly and thighs of bronze, depicted Alexander the Great and the Greeks. Alexander expanded his empire rapidly, but it didn't last long. It endured only from 363 to 332 BC.

The Legs

Following the bronze thighs were the legs of iron, which symbolized Rome, the strongest and fiercest of all the kingdoms to rule the world. The iron grip with which they controlled the world is recorded in the Bible as well as in world history (63 BC–AD 313).

The Toes

So where are we now in terms of world history and the image from Daniel 2?

We are currently in the section of iron and clay and are watching on global news networks as the ten toes are being formed. Every time you hear about the European Union, the United Nations, or NATO, think about the toes of iron and clay. While there are presently many more than ten nations involved in the world, we can see how many are starting to come together and how, through coalition and treaty, the number could be reduced rather quickly.

The Composition of the Statue

God was so precise in His revelation to Nebuchadnezzar and the interpretation through Daniel that, if you were to trace world history based on the statue's depictions, you would find that every detail of the image is totally accurate. And remember, Daniel gave this interpretation before anyone had heard of the kingdoms he was describing.

Consider even the hardness of the materials used in each section. Gold is soft and iron is hard. We see that as civilization progresses, so does the sophistication and destructiveness of weaponry. In Babylonian times, swords, spears, and shields made up the armory. Then, with the evolving civilizations, stronger and more durable weapons were formed. And finally, with our modernized warfare, we have created enough nuclear firepower to incinerate the entire planet.

Consider, too, the duality of the arms and legs. The two arms of silver are symbolic of the two nations, the allied Mede and Persian empires, that controlled their portion of the world after Babylon fell. The legs of iron depict the civil war that took place in the Roman Empire, which ultimately divided the once-unified republic into two separate kingdoms: the East and the West.

And then there's the composition of the toes, representing the world in our day. The toes are made of both iron and clay. One material is tough and the other is brittle. Even Daniel told Nebuchadnezzar that night so long ago, "As the toes of the feet were partly of iron and partly of clay, so the kingdom shall be partly strong and partly fragile" (Daniel 2:42).

What a perfect description of the world we're living in! Things just don't mix. There are certain countries that are strong militarily but weak economically. There are democracies and republics built on the idea that everyone is equal, and they certainly don't mix with the fundamentalist Islamic countries that practice Sharia law.

So the vision of a statue was no random dream by a hotheaded king. And its revelation was no lucky guess by a Jewish prophet. This was a pulling back of the curtain on the apocalypse as it pertained to what would happen to the kingdoms of the world up to and including the present day.

But the most powerful fact is that this dream tells us about the kingdom that will be the last one to rule over planet Earth.

THE STONE THAT DESTROYS THE STATUE

Daniel finished his description of Nebuchadnezzar's dream, saying, "Inasmuch as you saw that the stone was cut out of the mountain without hands, and that it broke in pieces the iron, the bronze, the clay, the silver, and the gold—the great God has made known to the king what will come to pass after this" (Daniel 2:45). The statue tells of the kingdoms of this world. The stone symbolizes the kingdom of heaven coming to earth.

Peter wrote to the first-century church a letter in which he described those who believed in Christ as "living stones" (1 Peter 2:5). Why? Because he said that Jesus Christ was the "chief cornerstone." Furthermore, "he who believes on Him will by no means be put to shame" (verse 6). He then quoted the prophet Isaiah and the Psalms to draw two more connections to the picture of Christ being represented in the symbol of a stone. Remember: "By the mouth of two or three witnesses . . ." (Matthew 18:16).

Daniel stated that the statue representing the kingdoms of world history would be utterly destroyed by a stone from the heavens. Peter said the stone that was rejected has become the chief cornerstone. In this book I'll be mentioning what the Bible says about some difficult times that lie directly ahead of us. But what we need to remember is that every God-defying government and leader will one day be supplanted by God's kingdom. It's a sure thing.

Go to any history book or encyclopedia with a time line recording global governments and thrones that have ruled the world, and you will see that Daniel wasn't just close in his interpretation of Nebuchadnezzar's statue; he was absolutely accurate in every detail. The kingdoms he described from Nebuchadnezzar's dream came and were replaced just as he said they would be. So it is only logical to conclude that what Daniel spoke regarding the uncut stone is true as well.

The kingdom of heaven is coming to the earth and will demolish all other governments, and once it is established, it will never end. Daniel confirms this truth by saying, "The dream is certain, and its interpretation is sure" (Daniel 2:45).

FOCUSING ON THE MAIN THING

A lot of debates take place when it comes to the end times and the apocalypse. There have been so many studies done, so many commentaries written, and so many sermons preached on this subject that I believe we sometimes are guilty of not listening to the music and only arguing about the notes on the page.

It's perplexing to me why most of the conversations and debates about the end times and prophecy seem to focus on the minor issues and not the major facts God has so graciously presented. Scholars want to argue about interpretations and doctrinal perspectives of certain singular aspects on the topic. My personal preference is to focus on the overwhelming major truths that world history verifies and that the Bible has proven time and time again.

The Bible is the only book that has accurately predicted prophecy after prophecy. Instead of focusing too much on the details of interpretations, we should celebrate the fact that our God is so wise that He can orchestrate all things from beginning to end. And with that being the case, He is certainly capable of handling any of the finer points of our lives and the world we live in as well.

Before you turn the page to the next chapter, consider this important question: If the interpretation has been pinpoint accurate thus far, then why wouldn't it continue to be so in the days to come?

Don't let this thought escape you: the Cornerstone is coming back to earth, and when He does, His kingdom will not end.

SIGNS OF THE END OF THE AGE

Tell us, when will these things be? And what will be the sign
of Your coming, and of the end of the age?

—Matthew 24:3

I was thirteen years old in the spring of 1992, traveling to Israel for the first time with my parents and a group of church members. We boarded a jumbo jet around midnight and began the transcontinental flight from New York's JFK to Ben Gurion Airport in Tel Aviv. When we arrived at the airport, we immediately boarded a bus and began to tour the city to help overcome jet lag.

Israel was not at all what I expected. Because of all the Bible stories I had heard throughout my childhood, I envisioned that I would be stepping back in time to a scene from our annual Christmas pageant. What I actually saw was a modern and prosperous nation. At that time I also didn't understand that I was quite literally walking on ground that was the fulfillment of prophecy and that there were many more of these prophecies yet to be fulfilled.

One of our first stops was the Israel Museum, which introduces visitors to the biblical land of Israel while also building a bridge to modern-day Israel. For me, one of the most impactful displays at the museum was a piece of art that opened my eyes to a historical fact I had never been exposed to. I am now in my late thirties, having obtained my education, including seminary, but to this day, the only way I learned this historical information was when I was outside classroom walls. (Isn't it amazing what isn't taught in school!)

The artwork was a rendering of the Arch of Titus, which sits in Rome and was built to honor the achievements of a general named Titus. It shows, in part, the results of this general's successful campaign in Judea from AD 66 to 70. It depicts robed men carrying artifacts from the temple in Jerusalem back to Rome. The sculpture captured the anguish and sorrow of the prisoners who are being taken with the sacred articles of the Holy City.

A sign with an arrow leading from the sculpture pointed to the next section of the museum, where I saw a brand-new word for me: "Diaspora." I asked my father, "What is the Diaspora?"

His answer was not short, but when he finished, I had begun to understand how the descendants of Abraham had been driven out of Israel and to all parts of Europe and the West by persecution and violence. I'll be getting to the Diaspora in another chapter, because it will be important to establish a pattern of hatred that will culminate in the end times. Here, though, we will look at the event that started it all, the event recorded in the Arch of Titus—the destruction of the temple in AD 70.

Seventy years before Titus's armies arrived on the Temple Mount, Jesus Christ told His disciples exactly what would happen from the day Titus destroyed the Holy City to the "appointed time" when He would return to earth to rule and reign. These signs provide a bridge from the generation living in Jesus's time to our own generation—the terminal generation.

Look Up!

Between the Triumphal Entry and the Crucifixion, the disciples and their Teacher engaged in several conversations. One is recorded in Matthew 24. It kicks off with these questions: "Tell us, when will these things be? And what will be the sign of Your coming, and of the end of the age?" (Matthew 24:3).

One of the amazing realities of God's Word is how deeply its principles can be applied. Matthew 24 provides a tremendous amount of truth that can be directly connected to the world we live in today. Often we pick the low-hanging fruit at the surface of the text and choose to let that be the primary application. While there is certainly nothing wrong with using Scripture in this manner, it is important to make sure you understand the context of the conversation so that, while you may apply the truth in a personal manner, you can also possess a full understanding of what the Scripture is communicating.

As we consider this section of Scripture, there will be moments when we can directly apply the truth that is revealed to our own time and the world we are living in. Then there are other portions of this text where we must look through the lens of history as it pertains to those Jesus was speaking with that day. In Matthew 24 Christ was speaking with His disciples, who were believers in and followers of Christ, but who were also exclusively Jewish. There are times when we forget the Jewishness of Jesus. He was a rabbi, trained in the Torah (first five books of the Hebrew Scriptures), and raised in a kosher home according to the law of Moses. In Scripture, He refers to the Jewish people as His brothers (see Matthew 25:40), and in this chapter He reveals truth about what will occur to them as a people from the first century until His return.

Some of the most powerful words written in all of Bible prophecy come from this conversation. It answers so many of the questions people ask when they start to worry about things they cannot control or change. I mentioned that I prefer to focus on the major themes rather than spend so much energy arguing about the details. Well, in Daniel's vision the major theme was the accuracy of prophecy; in this conversation the major theme is Jesus coming back.

Too often, when people hear about how close we are to the end, anxiety wraps its hand around their throat. After Jesus described a world with more trouble and tribulation than one would want to imagine, He told the disciples, "Now when these things begin to happen, look up and lift up your heads, because your redemption draws near" (Luke 21:28).

I want that to be the outcome of this entire study—for you, the reader, to "look up" and not hang your head because you are intimidated by the world that surrounds you. If you are a believer in Christ Jesus, whether you are Jewish or Gentile, you have a promise that is greater than the world around you. Lift up your head and be confident that Jehovah God is in control and He will take care of you. That is His promise, and He is faithful to do all that He has said He would. Don't let the darkness of evil overshadow the overwhelming fact that our hope is in the Light of the World.

NOT ONE STONE UPON ANOTHER

Jesus began the conversation from the mountainside by pointing to the glorious Temple Mount. Since it was the season of Passover, the temple was covered with thousands of pilgrims and worshippers. They had come to the very site Solomon had dedicated to God and prayed the prayers that Solomon said they would pray when he asked the Lord God Almighty to hear and answer them (see 2 Chronicles 6:20–21). This temple was no ordinary place. It was beautiful to behold, spiritually invigorating, and infused with energy and life that can only come from heaven above.

King Herod the Great, although a moral monster beyond what the English language can describe, was without question one of the world's most incredible construction managers. The engineering marvels he oversaw were achieved prior to modern machinery, and his workforce moved stones that to this day the world's most powerful cranes could not lift.

It took forty-six years for Herod's builders to accomplish the renovations that included the platform of the outer court, the retaining wall on the western side of the temple (which is the modern-day Wailing Wall), and the southern entrance, known today as the "southern steps." On the east side of the Temple Mount facing David's city and the Mount of Olives was the Eastern Gate, or Messiah's Gate. It was here that it was said the Messiah would enter when He comes to establish His throne. Today the gate is barricaded with stone and a Muslim cemetery. While it is not a tenet of the Islamic faith to believe that a Jewish Messiah will come, or that He will have a throne, they think they had better guard against Him anyway, just in case.

To the north, Herod built military barracks so that even in the most sacred of Jewish sites the high priest and worshippers would always be reminded that Rome was watching. While as a builder he was a genius, he was constantly worried about a possible assassination attempt or a would-be revolution. Due to his obsessions, he fortified himself everywhere and in every way he could with military strength, and the temple was no exception.

Jesus pointed to this massive and beautiful edifice and said, "Not one stone shall be left here upon another, that shall not be thrown down" (Matthew 24:2). He knew that in the minds of the disciples this was almost an impossible thought, yet He was telling them to expect the unexpected.

Jesus, looking through the eyes of prophecy, saw the Roman general Titus marching toward Jerusalem. It was under Titus's command that the Roman army began the siege of the Holy City during Passover in AD 70. They surrounded the city and built a wall. No one was allowed in or out. Tens of thousands were trapped inside with limited supplies. Some tried to dig tunnels to get out and they were blocked. Others, having sold all they had for gold coins, swallowed them and tried to escape in the night. When they were captured, however, the soldiers cut them open to remove the gold and then left their bodies to the vultures and wild dogs. It has been recorded that in one night no fewer than two thousand men and women were ripped open in this way.

The historian Josephus, who lived during Rome's destruction of Jerusalem, painstakingly recorded the gruesome cruelty that occurred during the siege that claimed nearly 1.1 million Jewish lives. In one account he detailed how "children pulled the very morsels that their fathers were eating out of their very mouths, and what was still more to be pitied, so did the mothers do as to their infants; and when those that were most dear were perishing under their hands, they were not ashamed to take from them the very last drops that might preserve their lives."[1]

Jesus not only told the disciples what was to come; He also warned the women of Jerusalem who were weeping for Him on the day of His crucifixion:

Daughters of Jerusalem, do not weep for Me, but weep for
yourselves and for your children. For indeed the days are
coming in which they will say, "Blessed are the barren, wombs
that never bore, and breasts which never nursed!" Then they
will begin "to say to the mountains, 'Fall on us!' and to the hills,
'Cover us!'" For if they do these things in the green wood, what
will be done in the dry? (Luke 23:28–31)

I have had many conversations with people who want to know if
Jesus was saying that in the end times it would be better not to have
children. I have even spoken with Millennial couples who attempt to
use this verse as a reason not to have children. That is a misuse of the
Scripture. Jesus was warning the citizens of Jerusalem, who walked by
the cross where He hung naked, beaten, and about to die, that if this is
what Rome did when there was no political trouble in Jerusalem, then
how much more horror would they unleash in a time of turmoil? "If
they [the Romans] do these things [the crucifixion] in the green wood
[good times], what will be done in the dry [time of turmoil]?"

Seventy years before it happened, Jesus saw the siege that would
inhumanely starve to death even the strongest of men. He spoke it, and
once again we see that the Bible is indeed accurate and that there is
more to come.

THE SIGN OF DECEPTION

The disciples asked, "When will these things be?" (Matthew 24:3). So
Jesus began by describing a spirit that would only intensify through to
the last days. "Take heed that no one deceives you," He said (verse 4).

The first-century church, after Christ's death and resurrection, was plagued with deception. Many false teachers claimed to be followers of Christ. Many simply denounced the faith because they could not believe that the rabbi from Nazareth had risen from the grave. Regardless of the source of deception, it was present then and it has only continued to increase from that time until this one.

Jesus referred to birth pains that will continue to increase until the moment of delivery. Deception is one of the signs of labor, and if the first-century church faced it, then today our whole world is simply saturated with it. We live in a world that is so full of deception that we have accepted feelings as facts; actual facts are no longer relevant. A person born as a biological man can choose to identify as a woman. And in our society, we are so much more interested in protecting feelings than we are in offending those who were actually born as women that we gave a man a Woman of the Year award![2]

Deception has penetrated almost every area of our society. In education, we are teaching our students that they were not created; they evolved. That's deception.

In church, pastors are standing behind the pulpit and using the words *love, grace,* and *acceptance* to condone behavior that God calls an abomination. We have deceived ourselves into believing that God's love and grace are so immense that He doesn't require a change in our conduct. That's deception. The question is not, "Does God love us?" That is a known fact. He loved us so much that He sent His only begotten Son to die for us. The question we should ask is, "Do we love God enough to change?"

Deception is everywhere. For example, we have a divorce rate in America that will affect as much as 40 or 50 percent of marriages, depending on whose research you use.[3] Now more than ever, young couples are choosing to just live together rather than get married, because they do not see a valid reason for marriage. Why? Deception. They grew up spending every other weekend with Dad, trying to decide whether they should call their new stepparent by his or her first name or actually take the plunge by calling this person Mom or Dad. The families they were born into began when the parents promised to love, cherish, and obey one another, but then they broke the vows they swore to keep. That is deception.

When Jesus warned the disciples that deception was going to mark the generation that would see His return, He could not have picked a word that more accurately and precisely captures the essence of our current culture: *deceived!*

The Signs of Wars and Disasters

Jesus continued to elaborate on the future. "And you will hear of wars and rumors of wars. See that you are not troubled; for all these things must come to pass, but the end is not yet" (Matthew 24:6).

If you were to calculate the number of years fought in wars from the time of Christ till now, you would come up with approximately eighteen hundred years of war and only two hundred years of peace.[4]

Said another way, we have spent about 90 percent of our time on earth fighting in one battle or another. From the siege of Jerusalem, to the Crusades of the Middle Ages, to the wars of Europe, to the conquest of the New World, and through WWI, WWII, Korea, Vietnam, Desert Storm, and Afghanistan, the world has always been waging a war or getting ready for the next one. Christ not only spoke of the wars that are mentioned above, but He also spoke of one that is yet to occur.

The coming battles are more fully described in Ezekiel 38–39, but in basic detail they tell how Russia is going to lead a coalition that includes Iran and other Islamic armies, along with select nations from Europe, such as Germany and Turkey, into battle against Israel. The Bible tells how, during that time, no one will assist Israel in her hour of trouble.

Here's how the fight will turn out. God said that on the day the enemies come against Israel—the moment their feet touch the sacred soil of His covenant land—God Almighty is going to unload on them in a manner no army has trained for. God will open up His attack on the invaders with an earthquake (see Ezekiel 38:19). This is a signature mark of God's. Do you recall how He judged the children of Israel when they were at Sinai worshipping the golden calf? The Bible records that the earth opened up and swallowed them (see Deuteronomy 11:6). Then consider what happened on the day Christ died: "The earth quaked, and the rocks were split" (Matthew 27:51). Similarly, Ezekiel says God will judge the armies that come against His people and His property, the land of Israel.

Then Ezekiel 38:21 states, "Every man's sword will be against his brother." We know this in modern warfare as *friendly fire*. Imagine a Russian, Iranian, Ethiopian, Egyptian, and German army attempting to communicate in battle where several thousand men have been killed in a sudden, massive earthquake. It would be highly possible for them to engage in friendly fire.

God has done this before. Remember Gideon in the book of Judges? He faced his enemies and alarmed them so much that, while retreating in fear, they began to fight one another (see Judges 7:22). History repeats itself.

Then, as a finishing touch, God proclaims in Ezekiel 38:22, "I will rain down on him . . . great hailstones, fire, and brimstone." God lets us know in the final verse that when He is done fighting this fight, "I will be known in the eyes of many nations. Then they shall know that I am the LORD" (verse 23).

People ask me on a regular basis what will cause our world to wake up. When will we stop and consider how far we are from where God wants us to be?

I assure you, when the world sees the news coverage that I just described, that Ezekiel described, and that Jesus spoke about, there won't be an empty seat in any church from San Antonio, Texas, to Sydney, Australia!

There are many people who believe that the battle described in Ezekiel 38 is the Battle of Armageddon. It is not. The Battle of Armageddon is going to make the war in Ezekiel look like a cakewalk at a county fair; blood will run for miles "up to the horses' bridles" during the Battle of Armageddon (Revelation 14:20).

Jesus stated in Matthew 24:7 that "nation will rise against nation." The word translated "nation" is *ethnos,* and in this context it means "groups of people." For all the talk about "inclusion" and "unity" in our society, there has never been a time when groups of people have had greater contention with each other than now. Riots in major cities are drawn with racial lines. The radical Islamic army that is marching across the Middle East is crucifying, beheading, and torturing people along the way who are not of their *ethnos.*

Jesus also referred to fighting "kingdom against kingdom" (verse 7). Here He was speaking of world wars.

Jesus then described natural disasters. He concluded with, "All these are the beginning of sorrows" (verse 8). Remember the birth pains? It is when you see these signs that the birth pains have begun.

The end is not yet. Once they start, however, they will only get more intense up to the moment the One you are expecting arrives. These birth pangs really began two thousand years ago when the church began. They have continued ever since and are getting noticeably more intense in our day.

A CRESCENDO OF HATRED

Remember the former things of old,
For I am God, and there is no other;
I am God, and there is none like Me,
Declaring the end from the beginning,
And from ancient times things that are not yet done.

—Isaiah 46:9–10

I n the last chapter, we began looking at the prophetic talk Jesus gave to the disciples on the Mount of Olives. The tension must have begun to increase within the group as Christ described a world so different from the one the disciples were expecting.

Jesus continued His conversation with the disciples by making nine statements, each beginning with the word "then." These statements create a sequential order of events that can be traced throughout history, and much like the dream Daniel interpreted, they not only prove how accurate the Word of God is but also give us confidence regarding what it states for the future.

In this chapter we're going to focus only on the first of the nine "then" statements: "Then they will deliver you up to tribulation and kill you, and you will be hated by all nations for My name's sake" (Matthew

24:9). Who was Jesus referring to when He said "you"? Let's use some basic deductive reasoning to answer the question. Consider that Jesus was a Jewish rabbi, and He was talking to His disciples, who were also Jewish. It seems logical then, that verse 9 describes what will happen to the Jewish people when they are faced with anti-Semitism on a global scale.

What we find when we interrogate history regarding its treatment of the Jewish people is that anti-Semitism has flared up again and again. In fact, it has never really disappeared. I'm going to show you some sad and troubling examples to sensitize you to the pervasiveness of the problem. The underlying point is that today anti-Semitism is reaching a point where the nation of Israel's very existence is at risk, with her enemies acquiring weapons of mass destruction and with the protection of her friends weakening. A key part of the end times is warfare on a massive scale centered on Israel. As anti-Semitism is reaching its peak, conditions are becoming ripe for this prophecy of the end to come true.

HISTORY'S SHAME

When Jesus told His disciples, "Then they will deliver you up to tribulation and kill you, and you will be hated by all nations for My name's sake" (Matthew 24:9), He was speaking about all that would occur to the Jewish people from that day until this one. After the birth of the Christian church, religious leaders began to spread false doctrine that the Jews were the "Christ killers." This led to widespread anti-Semitism. The problem with this evil accusation is that if any group of people or government could truly be responsible for the death of Christ, then His death wasn't a willing sacrifice. Yet this basic fact didn't keep the lie from slithering through the Christianized nations of the world.

The Crusades

Consider the Crusades of the Middle Ages. Without question, they were a major birth pain of war, with nation rising against nation. In 1096 the first crusade entered Jerusalem. The Crusaders claimed that their purpose in marching from Europe to the Holy City was to reclaim the land for Christ. Yet, as with the Roman legions before them, their purpose was far from holy and their motivation anything but pure. Having been given absolution from sin before the journey began, the Crusaders engaged in every vile act imaginable, raping, pillaging, burning, stealing, and murdering all the way to Jerusalem and back again.

One account of what occurred during the Crusades gives a terrifying glimpse of the horrors inflicted upon the Jews. It was during the first crusade, as the conquering army entered Jerusalem, that frightened women and children ran into a synagogue for safety. More than nine hundred innocent souls filled the building. Then the moral monsters who were on the other side of the door set the structure on fire and marched around the blazing walls, singing "Christ We Adore Thee."[1] These were not holy men. They did not represent Christ in any way! They represented the anti-Semitic spirit that Christ warned of in Matthew 24 and that is still present in the world today.

Jesus said, "For My name's sake." Although the Crusaders were using the name of Christ in vain, they were fulfilling the words that were spoken on the Mount of Olives down to the last letter. The Crusaders were commissioned by the religious leaders in Rome to kill those whom they falsely accused of killing Christ, while totally ignoring the fact that Christ clearly stated, "No one takes [My life] from Me, but I lay it down of Myself" (John 10:18). Sadly, they were not the last to engage in this reprehensible behavior.

The Inquisition

Fast-forward to the year 1478. That was when the Jewish population in Spain began to face what is known as the Spanish Inquisition, the most infamous of many forms of inquisition that were used to persecute Jews and others over a period of centuries within Christendom. The Inquisitor General, Torquemada, was sent to Spain for the purpose of removing all Jews from Spain, be it by forced conversion, torture, murder, or expulsion. Once again, people using the name of Christ persecuted the Jews in the exact fashion foretold in Matthew 24.

Propaganda booklets were printed and passed out on how to spot a Jew. Those who were simply accused of being Jewish were turned over to the inquisitor and put on trial. They were tortured, pulled to pieces on racks, and burned at the stake. In 1492 Queen Isabella and King Ferdinand issued the Edict of Expulsion ordering all Jews to leave Spain, and an estimated two hundred thousand were expelled. Thousands were killed during this time for being Jewish . . . and their murderers bore the sign of the cross.

But Roman Catholics don't bear all the blame for the injustices inflicted upon the Jews. Protestants must accept their share as well.

Martin Luther

Around the same period when the Spanish Inquisition was in operation, a German priest began a movement that swept the world and shook the Church of Rome. It was called the Reformation, and it was founded on a simple biblical principle: "The just will live by faith." The prophet Habakkuk first wrote these words to the Jewish people to encourage them to continue in the faith of their father Abraham. Later, the apostle Paul would quote these words, speaking from the perspective of someone who was Jewish and who had received the revelation of Jesus Christ.[2] Martin Luther was convinced that the persecuted Jews of Europe would see the light and embrace his thesis and the Reformation movement itself. But they did not.

One of the major theological chasms to cross was that Christianity spoke of God in terms of three Persons, as a triune being. Jews had been taught, "The Lord our God is one," and had trouble reconciling that with the Trinity. At first, Luther had recognized the Jewish contribution to Christianity.[3] But once he realized that the Jews would not follow him, he became incensed and foolishly launched an assault on those to whom God had promised,

I will bless those who bless you,
And I will curse him who curses you. (Genesis 12:3)

His venomous doctrine was anti-Semitism at its worst. In his booklet *The Jews and Their Lies,* he gave such vile instructions as the following:
- "First to set fire to their synagogues or schools and to bury and cover with dirt whatever will not burn."
- "Second, I advise that their houses also be razed and destroyed."
- "Third, I advise that all their prayer books and Talmudic writings, in which such idolatry, lies, cursing and blasphemy are taught, be taken from them."
- "Fourth, I advise that their rabbis be forbidden to teach henceforth on pain of loss of life and limb."
- "Fifth, I advise that safe conduct on the highways be abolished completely for the Jews."

- "Sixth, I advise that usury be prohibited to them, and that all cash and treasure of silver and gold be taken from them."
- "Seventh, I commend putting a flail, an ax, a hoe, a spade, a distaff, or a spindle into the hands of young, strong Jews and Jewesses and letting them earn their bread in the sweat of their brow, as was imposed on the children of Adam."
- "We must drive them out like mad dogs."

He encouraged others to rid the country of what he called "the unbearable, devilish burden of the Jews."[4]

Martin Luther delivered his last sermon on February 18, 1546, just days before his death. It was "entirely devoted to the obdurate Jews, whom it was a matter of great urgency to expel from all German territory," according to historian Léon Poliakov.[5] Luther took his last breath on earth—choosing to spew his anti-Semitic poison to the end—and then stood in front of the God of Abraham, Isaac, and Jacob and a Jewish rabbi named Jesus.

The Holocaust

If all that Luther had instructed was not done in his lifetime, it was certainly carried out in Nazi Germany. Adolf Hitler, the supreme leader of the Nazi Party, studied theology from a young age. He loved and agreed fully with Luther's writings about how to handle the Jews. Just look at how many of Luther's directives Hitler implemented.

- Hitler burned their synagogues.
- He confiscated their homes and possessions.
- He forbade them from practicing their faith, saying their prayers, reading the Torah, or keeping the Sabbath holy.

- He forced them to be registered and labeled, and prevented them from leaving the country.
- He pushed them into ghettoes, rounded them up, and put those who could to work, and those who could not, to death in gas chambers and in front of firing squads.
- His purpose was to rid the world of the Jewish "burden."

In November of 1938, on the anniversary of Martin Luther's birthday, Hitler launched a massive and violent operation against the Jews. Seven years later, more than six million Jews—one million of whom were children—were murdered in the Holocaust.

Israel at Risk Today

Many want to dismiss anti-Semitism as effectively coming to an end after the Holocaust. If only that were true! Sadly, anti-Semitism is alive and well today. Remember Matthew 24:9: the Jewish people "will be hated by all nations." History repeats itself.

During the Obama administration, America treated Israel—one of the nation's allies—with more animosity than it did its enemies. The president and the State Department were constantly pressuring Israel to make concessions, surrender land, and cease and desist growth within their own borders. America has given hundreds of millions of dollars and pledged more to Israel's Islamic sworn enemies, one of whose goals is the destruction of Israel. Their cause is being funded by American taxpayer dollars and used in the effort to capture and control the city of Jerusalem and crush the nation of Israel.[6]

When Jesus said "all nations," He meant *all nations*. Even the United States of America persecutes the Jewish people.

Every word Jesus spoke has come to pass over the last twenty centuries concerning His brothers, the Jews. Every detail, from Daniel and

Nebuchadnezzar to Jesus and the disciples on the Mount of Olives, has pulled back the veil of history and has demonstrated beyond a shadow of a doubt this truth: we are living in those days when Jesus Himself said, "Then the end will come" (Matthew 24:14).

THE GREATEST MIRACLE OF OUR TIME

Who has ever heard of such a thing?
Who has ever seen such things?
Can a country be born in a day
or a nation be brought forth in a moment?

—Isaiah 66:8, NIV

The word *miracle* is applied to lots of things that are anything but. We see something remarkable and yet totally within the realm of possibility, and we quickly claim, "It's a miracle!"

Our favorite team wins the championship in the last game of the season on a final shot from half court. "It's a miracle!"

A golfer hits a hole in one from two hundred yards away. "It's a miracle!"

You make it through a day's travel with three connecting flights and no delays and no lost luggage. "It's a miracle!"

While all of these situations are rare and wonderful moments to celebrate, they are far from miraculous. They may indeed have been highly unlikely, but they were not impossible. They have been done before and for certain they will happen again.

But if you really want to see a miracle, then look at the modern-day

State of Israel. Even the prophet Isaiah had a difficult time understanding what he heard when God told him that a nation would be born in a day. But it happened. And several years later, Israel took another miraculous step toward its apocalyptic destiny when it once again took over sovereignty of Jerusalem and the Temple Mount.

This is history we need to know, because it is one of the clearest, as well as most miraculous, indications of the nearness of the end in our own time.

Israel's Rebirth-Day

In previous chapters we spoke about the Diaspora and the persecution that has afflicted the Jewish people all over the world for centuries. The moment that the temple was destroyed in AD 70, the children of Israel in essence lost their land. They were no longer in control of their destiny. They had no sovereignty and were subject to Gentile rule, whether in peace or in strife. The land itself was still their inheritance, but the flag that flew over it was not their flag.

It's a twisting of this history that causes some to say that Israel today is usurping land that really belongs to the Palestinians. It is important to keep the facts straight and to the point, and the point is that the Palestinians have never had a claim on the land of Israel. That land was created by God and given to Abraham, Isaac, and Jacob.[1]

So how did the situation get where it is today?

In AD 130, the Roman emperor Hadrian decided that he would insult the Jews for their rebellious resistance to Rome by ordering Judea to be renamed Palaestina on maps. He chose that name in tribute to the Philistines, the Old Testament enemies of the Jewish people. That name stuck as the power struggle in the Middle East continued.

By the twentieth century, the kingdom of Great Britain controlled the territory of Israel, which was still not a nation. Israel was under the British crown and was a place where Jews came from all over the Mediterranean basin, as well as North Africa and the Middle East, seeking a better life than what they were afforded in the surrounding Islamic nations. It continued to be called by the Roman-issued name until a miracle occurred in 1948.

When World War II ended, the survivors of the Holocaust were finally free to leave the death camps where they had been sent to be systematically slaughtered. But where were they to go and where would they live? Many returned to the villages and towns they had lived in for years, only to find that their houses were destroyed or another family was occupying them. This matter of homelessness was not an easy one to resolve. Yet something had to be done.

On May 14, 1948, under the leadership of the first Israeli prime minister, David Ben-Gurion, the announcement was made: "We hereby proclaim the establishment of the Jewish state in Palestine, to be called Israel."[2] The ceremony was broadcast over the radio to the nations of the world. At an East Texas home, sitting at a small kitchen table with a radio in the middle of it, my then-eight-year-old father heard the announcement and watched his father, my grandfather, say with misty eyes and a voice filled with emotion, "This is the most significant day in Bible history in eighteen hundred years."

A nation was literally born in a day. These were the exact words God had given to Isaiah three thousand years prior, and they had come to pass. The prophet wrote the headlines before the world even knew what a newspaper was—it was God's way of reminding all who were willing to take notice that the God of Abraham, Isaac, and Jacob is alive and still keeping His promises.

WHEN AMERICA WAS ISRAEL'S FRIEND

A side note of history that isn't often taught but that is worth mentioning is the fact that the United States of America was the first country whose government officially recognized the new nation of Israel. America did this on the very day Israel proclaimed its independence. And this was not a small token or just a nod of approval. It was, in fact, a massive endorsement representing a huge political risk.

There was no question that, coming out of the battlefields of WWII, the United States was the new global superpower. The most powerful man on the face of the earth sat in the Oval Office, and despite receiving great pressure from the U.S. State Department not to do it, and ignoring the threats of the Arab nations who were infuriated at the idea of an Israeli state, President Harry S. Truman let the world know that the United States of America stood with Israel.

Recall the words that Daniel spoke when he received the interpretation of Nebuchadnezzar's dream:

> He removes kings and raises up kings;
> He gives wisdom to the wise
> And knowledge to those who have understanding.
>   (Daniel 2:21)

President Truman was a man whom the Lord called to occupy a place of influence at a key moment in history and gave him the wisdom and knowledge to support this new nation of Israel.

"He was a student and believer in the Bible since his youth. From his reading of the Old Testament he felt the Jews derived a legitimate historical right to Palestine, and he sometimes cited such biblical lines as Deuteronomy 1:8: 'Behold, I have given up the land before you; go in and take possession of the land which the Lord hath sworn unto your fathers, to Abraham, to Isaac, and to Jacob.'"[3]

Truman once said, "I had faith in Israel even before it was established. I knew it was based on the love of freedom, which has been the guiding star of the Jewish people since the days of Moses."[4]

Think about it: If the United States had not been the global power that led the world against the Axis forces and defeated Germany and Japan, and if Truman had not been in that place of power on that specific day, then the story would have been a different one than we read today. Yet, in God's awesome sovereignty, when He wanted the dead, dry, and scattered bones of Ezekiel's vision to come back to life (see Ezekiel 37:1–14), He placed the right man in the right place at the right time. It was, without a doubt, a miracle.

SIX DAYS TO ANOTHER MIRACLE

Even though the land of Israel declared its independence in 1948, there was still a prophetic matter that needed to come to pass before the followers of Jesus Christ could start looking up for His reappearance. The issue? Jerusalem was still under Gentile control, and yet the city of David (Jerusalem), according to Scripture, was supposed to be under the control of the Jews when Jesus returned.

When Jesus prophetically said, "The times of the Gentiles are fulfilled" (Luke 21:24), He was referring to the city of Jerusalem being under Gentile control. And then, once that time is over, He stated in verse 32, "Assuredly, I say to you, this generation will by no means pass away till all things take place."

But before "all things take place," Israel must endure more

hardships. Understand that conflict is nothing new to the Jewish people. Just days after their independence was declared, they were in a battle that lasted a full year. It was the beginning of armed conflict and threats toward the nation that still rage on today. This, too, was foretold.

> See how your enemies are astir,
>> how your foes rear their heads.
> With cunning they conspire against your people;
>> they plot against those you cherish.
> "Come," they say, "let us destroy
>> them as a nation,
> that the name of Israel be
>> remembered no more." (Psalm 83:2–4, NIV)

Forces of evil on this earth hate the nation of Israel because God loves His chosen people.

Nevertheless, nineteen years after the founding of modern Israel, the nation endured a great test—and scored a great victory. As if the birth of a nation in a single day wasn't miraculous enough, the events that happened during the Six-Day War were nothing less than supernatural! In those six days, some of the most remarkable events in the history of the world took place.

On May 15, 1967, Egypt to the south, Syria to the north, and Jordan to the east, along with Lebanon and Iraq, joined forces to "destroy them as a nation" (Psalm 83:4, NIV). An estimated 465,000 Arab troops, with 2,800 tanks and 800 aircraft, were committed to putting an end to Israel during this conflict.[5] Six days of fighting later, here is what a German journalist recorded:

Nothing like this has happened in history. A force including 1000 tanks, hundreds of artillery cannons, many rockets and fighter jets, and a hundred thousand soldiers armed from the head to toe was destroyed in two days in an area covering hundreds of kilometers filled with reinforced outpost and installations. And this victory was carried out by a force that lost many soldiers and much equipment, positions, and vehicles. No military logic or natural cause can explain the monumental occurrence.[6]

King Hussein of Jordan was the first to offer a cease-fire. He realized that if the fighting continued as it was, the coalition's plan to crush Israel would backfire and Israel would actually wind up with more land than they started with. His greatest concern was the city of Jerusalem, and he wasn't wrong to worry about it. By the end of the six days, the Old City, the Western Wall, and the Temple Mount were under Jewish control. For the first time in nearly nineteen hundred years, the prayers from the Torah and the psalms of praise were sung on the Temple Mount, the same location where Jesus had told His disciples that "not one stone shall be left here upon another" (Matthew 24:2).

Although parts of Jerusalem and the Temple Mount have been negotiated for use by the local Muslim community, it still belongs to the Israeli government, which has official sovereignty over it. Jerusalem belongs to the Jewish people and is a pivotal city in the plan of God. But there are still others who want to rule over it.

The clockwork progression of events being set up for the final conflicts of history surrounding Israel moved forward another notch. The stunning reality of modern Israel's presence in the world guarantees that the end is not far off.

THE SETTING IS READY

Every time you hear the word *Israel* on the evening news, you are listening to someone giving testimony to a miracle. Each time you hear people talk about the city of Jerusalem, they are reminding you that every word and promise of God is true. There is no way to see the Star of David flying on a flag above the wall of the Old City and not take what Christ said to heart. "Heaven and earth will pass away, but My words will by no means pass away" (Matthew 24:35).

The day that the church received the Holy Spirit in the upper room was the day the labor pains of the end times began. When Jerusalem returned to Jewish control, those pains intensified exponentially. All the signs have been fulfilled. You have a reason to look up and start watching the heavens, because the expected one is about to arrive.

HOW THE FINANCIAL DOMINOES WILL FALL

The love of money is a root of all kinds of evil,
for which some have strayed from the faith in their greediness,
and pierced themselves through with many sorrows.

—1 Timothy 6:10

Who can argue that an intense hunger for money is a hallmark of our day? Not that money is inherently bad, but it's terribly risky when people put their sense of security and significance in their financial well-being instead of in God. So in this chapter and the two that follow, I want to show how economic realities we see before us today are preparing for evil forces to take power in this world.

The financial dominoes are lining up right now. It will only take a nudge at the right moment for them all to topple over.

THE COMING FINANCIAL DOOMSDAY

I was staying at the Hilton Hotel in downtown Louisville, Kentucky, getting dressed for the first day of a week-long National Quartet Convention. I was looking forward to seeing old friends, meeting new ones, and hearing great gospel music. While I was going through my morning routine, the local news station carried the first reports of a commuter plane that, for some unknown reason, apparently had crashed into one of the World Trade Center towers.

As the morning of September 11 unfolded, the news reports that were pouring in let us know that the world we went to sleep in was gone forever. We were now facing an enemy like none we had ever known before. Terrorists brought down two towers that represented the financial strength of the United States, capitalism, and the West. They struck the Pentagon, sticking their finger in the eye of our military might. They had intended to hit the White House but failed to do so when the brave passengers of Flight 93 sacrificially resisted. At the end of the day, the stock market was closed and movers and shakers in the world's economy took a pause from commerce to catch their breath and see what was going to happen next.

Everyone has a story about that fateful day. Many went through things so heartbreaking that, more than a decade and a half later, the wounds have yet to heal. I wish with all that is in me that I could say that was the last time terrorism would interrupt our lives, but we all know too well that has not been the case. And someday soon there will be another headline about a much bigger attack, and unlike what we saw with the tragedy of 9/11, the markets will not reopen, the economy will not recover, and the financial doomsday that many have warned about will be here.

Then what?

In Matthew 24:11 Jesus said, "Then many false prophets will rise up and deceive many." Throughout history there have indeed been many who made the false claim that they were the Messiah. The most horrific and vile of these false prophets is yet to come, but with every hour that passes, his arrival is getting closer. And the economic chaos that will reign will pave the way for him to take power.

The World's Wicked Economic "Savior"

It's not my intention in this book to go into detail about the Antichrist and the evil he will bring to the world. But we need to take a look at this figure briefly to see how our culture, and in particular our financial culture, right now is taking shape to make the Antichrist's job easier.

Daniel the prophet had his own vision years after he interpreted Nebuchadnezzar's dream. Rather than a statue with a head of gold and feet of iron and clay, he saw a series of beasts (see Daniel 7:1–8). Each beast was unique. While they had certain common features, they also had aspects that were far from normal. They included a lion with wings, a bear with one leg shorter than the others and three rib bones in his mouth, a leopard with four heads and wings, and then a fourth beast, "dreadful and terrible, exceedingly strong" (Daniel 7:7). This fourth beast had ten horns.

The beasts that Daniel described are a panorama of global powers that will rule the earth. Like the levels of Nebuchadnezzar's statue, these beasts appear in a sequential order and are accurately depicted. The dreadful and terrible beast with ten horns paints the same prophetic picture of the ten toes of clay and iron coming out of the fragments of the Roman Empire. The features of the beast give greater details of the characteristics of each kingdom, which once again confirms the accuracy of Bible prophecy.

"I was considering the horns," Daniel said, "and there was another horn, a little one" (verse 8). This little horn represents a leader who is going to come to power. We may not know his name, but his title has been clear for centuries: the Antichrist.

When you consider what the Bible says about the outcome of the Antichrist's global dictatorship and cruelty to anyone who resists him, some may ask how he could ever come to power. The answer is simple. The world will beg him to lead.

He will not walk into a room with a name tag that says, "Hello. My name is Antichrist, and I'm the one they warned you about." He will come to power when the world is in economic chaos. When the news flash tells the world that all of the money they thought they had is gone, and when the nations of the world beg him to solve this global economic problem that they have created over a period of decades, then it will be as Daniel prophesied. "He shall cause craft to prosper" (Daniel 8:25, KJV), meaning he will pave the way for a thriving commerce.[1]

This is the moment in prophecy when history, culture, and the economy collide. Today the stage is set for this global leader to take his place, all due to the volatile and manipulated global financial markets. The world has known its series of financial downturns and depressions over the centuries. At times they have affected major industries, nations, and even whole regions of the world. But never in history have the conditions been so ripe as they are now for an economic crash to take place all over the world at the same time.

THE VULNERABILITY OF TODAY'S INTERCONNECTED GLOBAL ECONOMY

The world has never been as globally connected as it is now, making nations no longer financially independent or sovereign. For more than forty years, leaders of the world's most economically powerful nations have met in the "G" meetings to discuss how to keep the global economies stabilized. Among other things, at these meetings they have proposed, argued, rejected, and defended the idea of issuing a single global currency.

The euro has been an experiment in recent history to see if multiple countries, with a wide range of economic strengths, can work together off a common currency. The results have been mixed, to say the least. The stronger economic powers are not pleased with how the less financially stable countries affect their ability to buy and trade internationally. Remember, iron and clay don't mix.

Consider Britain's vote to leave the then-twenty-eight-nation bloc known as the EU (European Union). Within the borders of Britain, there were two factions, one yelling "Stay!" and the other yelling "Go!" Outside the borders, nations were greatly concerned about what the exit would do to the rest of the world. Why? Because like it or not, we are all in this together.

In May 2016, *USA Today* stated, "The International Monetary Fund and the U.S. Federal Reserve Board see the British exit (Brexit) as the single biggest threat to the global economy already struggling with anemic growth."[2] How did we get to this point? And what do decisions made by British citizens—or by other peoples around the world—have to do with soccer moms and blue-collar dads in America?

Angela Merkel, chancellor of Germany, and other European leaders have called for a "superstate" where previously independent nations would join together in order to be able to create financial stability.[3] What does a nation have to do to be a part of this proposed superstate?

1. Give up its currency and use the currency of the new state.
2. Give up its military and contribute troops to the fighting forces of the new state.

3. Give up its national borders, since the land is no longer theirs.

4. Give up its sovereignty and pledge allegiance to the superstate.

Even if Merkel's idea doesn't become a reality right away, you can be certain this won't be the last time this concept is presented. Today it's an idea to be considered; soon it will be a force that will rule the world and attempt to destroy anything and everything that would oppose it. Why?

Proverbs 22:7 states, "The borrower is servant to the lender." When you borrow, then every dime you earn belongs to the one you borrowed it from until that debt is repaid. The same can be said of nations. The economically strong nations of Europe can force their will over other nations that owe them significant sums of money, because if they were to require immediate payment, the weaker nations would financially collapse.

Let's apply this example in a more personal setting before we continue to expand the concept to the global markets.

Debt Slavery

In most households today, credit cards are a common means of acquisition. Some say credit is there in case of emergency; others consider it a necessity for business; and others simply enjoy the idea of getting what they want today and paying for it tomorrow. Regardless of why, every time you lay a credit card on the counter and sign your name, you are using money that is not yours and agreeing in writing to pay off the loan in days to come.

So let's say you have a job that pays you $1,000 a week, and you have expenses that cost you $700 a week. You have on average $300 left over from every paycheck, or $1,200 a month. But your credit card says that you can acquire $3,500 worth of merchandise and all you have to do is swipe and sign. So you think, *Why should I use my extra $300 when I could use the credit card company's $3,500?*

Sounds reasonable. But the problem with this kind of financial behavior is that you have just decided that for the next three months your expendable income belongs to Visa, Mastercard, or American Express. For at least the next ninety days, they are going to look forward to your paycheck more than you will. In many cases, people pay only the minimum amount required on the debt, which means the interest charged by the credit card company becomes a runaway train filled with money problems and with results that are devastating.

That's how debt works on a personal level. It is essentially the same on national, international, and global levels. The borrower is slave to the lender.

For example, the United States has been piling up debt for years. Rather than making an agreement with a credit card company, this nation has been saying that future generations will pay for what we agree to offer today. We can't afford to pay for a government health care plan, or bank bailouts, or car companies that have not managed their business well, but if we print more money today, then our descendants for the next 150 years will have to find a way to pay for it. The promises that have been made by one generation of leaders are more than we can afford to pay in the next two hundred years (if the world should continue turning on its axis that long).

The United States has primarily borrowed from the Chinese, who own more of our financial resources than we can afford for them to have. We may not want to admit it, but we are sending more of what we produce in income over there than we are keeping here. China is our creditor, and like the credit card companies in the earlier example, they look forward to our payday more than we do.

So how do major financial decisions made in foreign countries impact soccer moms and blue-collar dads in the United States?

When the next global financial crisis occurs, there will be only two choices for the United States to make. The first option will be to print more money, which will lead to inflation: the more dollars printed, the less each dollar is worth in your pocket. This means the price of gas and groceries will go up, because what five dollars could buy yesterday it cannot buy today. That's the part that will impact the soccer mom. And then in addition, our creditors, primarily China, may decide they no longer want our money, because the more of it we print, the less value it has for them. And that's where things could really get messy.

Printing more money has been the answer of choice for years because it artificially supports an economy that otherwise would decline. It alleviates fear and uncertainty, which are bad for business. But this is only a temporary fix, one that has long-term impacts that are potentially devastating. When you study the history of inflation in financial markets around the world, you see pictures of wheelbarrows full of money being traded for a sack of potatoes. Why? Because the potatoes have a significant value, while the currency in that wheelbarrow has very little. We already are aware that the buying power of the American dollar is decreasing every day, yet our leaders are doing nothing to stop it, and as a matter of fact, they are continuing to make it weaker and leaving the consequences to you, your children, and your grandchildren.

The other option America has regarding the next global economic crisis is that we could simply decide to stop spending on what we cannot afford. That would presumably mean spending cuts in Social Security, health care, welfare, and the funding of special-interest groups such as Planned Parenthood. While that is by no means the complete list of what the government currently spends our money on, all are without question expensive and definitely hot topics intensely debated and defended by different sides. If the American people think they would be forced to sacrifice what a politician promised when they voted for him or her, it could cause a tidal wave of social upheaval and unrest, or worse—anarchy.

Is this a problem? Yes, a very real one! Who's going to solve it? According to Daniel, he is the little horn and he will "cause craft to prosper." Stay tuned. We haven't heard the last of this character.

A God Bigger Than the Whole World's Wealth

If you're starting to feel scared, let me remind you that God is still sovereign and in control. He wants you to understand the times, but He doesn't want you to fear the future. In fact, if you are a believer in Jesus Christ, you won't even be here when the real tribulation finally hits.

We are told in the prophecies of Isaiah that the Lord's ways are not our ways, that His thoughts are not our thoughts (see Isaiah 55:8–9). His approach to accomplishing His will is so contrary to the ways of man that we often find it difficult in our limited understanding to see how the events taking place in the world around us could possibly be used by God, and yet He is faithful to make all things work together for the good of those who love Him (see Romans 8:28). This is true for the mega-economic upheavals that lie ahead. It is also true—as we will see in the next chapter—for an environmental viewpoint that will further help to hand the Antichrist the power he craves.

ENVIRONMENTAL HOSTAGES

[They] exchanged the truth of God for the lie,
and worshiped and served the creature rather
than the Creator, who is blessed forever.
Amen.

—Romans 1:25

In the previous chapter, I mentioned the convergence of history, prophecy, and culture. Well, nothing could better reflect that than what we see happening when it comes to the environment and how companies, private citizens, and the economy are being held hostage by what many world leaders claim is the greatest threat of our time—global warming.

It is not my intention to debate the truth or falsehood of global warming. But I do want to point out the fact that many are using climate change to try to increase governmental control over the lives of citizens. This is nothing short of a sign of the end times because, just as the Antichrist will need to portray himself as the savior of a world in economic crisis, so he needs people who are used to submitting themselves to an all-powerful government.

ENCROACHMENT

Let me begin by saying that I love nature and creation. God entrusted the world to man, and one of the first responsibilities that He gave to Adam was to tend to the garden and be a steward of what He had created (see Genesis 1:28–30; 2:15). Entire sections of Scripture show how God held generations accountable for what they did to abuse the land and the natural resources He made. Remember, "The earth is the LORD's, and everything in it, the world, and all who live in it" (Psalm 24:1, NIV). So not only is God a Creator, but He is also a conservationist.

Yet there must be balance, and now more than ever, our world is out of balance. Claims made in the name of environmentalism have become extreme. We have been told that the average temperatures of Earth's atmosphere and its oceans are gradually increasing and that the impact will be catastrophic. Descriptions of cities under water, islands covered by the sea, ice caps melting and drowning hundreds of thousands have all been given as examples of what global warming could do if it's not stopped.

The Obama administration took unprecedented action on environmental issues. In June 2013, the president gave a speech in which he made several things clear.[1] Climate change, in his opinion, is not a distant threat, but rather we are already feeling its impact across the country. He stated that we need to take drastic steps to cut carbon gas emissions from the corporate, municipal, and private sectors. This means that cities, businesses, and even *you* should be regulated by the government in order to protect the planet for future generations.

It all sounds reasonable when spoken, but what does it look like when applied? These steps will require that the U.S. government, particularly the Environmental Protection Agency, increase its scope of authority and begin to regulate more than it already does. Don't let this thought escape you: the larger the government gets, the smaller your freedoms become. Under the canopy of *green energy,* you will begin to see greater and more costly restrictions placed on what type of car you can drive, what kinds of fixtures you can have in your home, how you will get to and from work, and so on.

I know it may all sound Orwellian and too much of a stretch to believe, but if you take a step back and look, you can see it's already happening around you. Consider the ethanol debate.

THE CORN SWINDLE

Ethanol is a by-product of corn and is a potent alcohol that can be used as fuel for motor vehicles. In recent years, ethanol production has created a boon for corn growers as they have another place to market their product. In states where farming is a major source of revenue, ethanol production is certainly big business. All that aside, though, does it really help the environment?

The facts say no. According to a report released in 2014 by the United Nations Intergovernmental Panel on Climate Change, while ethanol burns much cleaner than petroleum-based fuels, if you consider what it takes to grow the crops and process the ethanol, it doesn't benefit the environment much at all. Another group—the International Institute for Sustainable Development—likewise stated that the net climate benefit from replacing petroleum fuels with biofuels like ethanol is basically zero. Other studies have reported that as land dedicated to fuel production increases, the land used for food production decreases, which leads to the conclusion that biofuels may cause more harm than good.[2]

In 2014, more than sixty nations adopted biofuel mandates, and the competition between corn for ethanol and corn for food has now become a moral issue. The less food that is produced, the greater the price will be on the store shelf. The first to be affected by this trend will be those with lower incomes who must make every dollar count and for whom the tug-of-war between gas and groceries is real.

Look at these numbers. "In 2000, over 90% of the U.S. corn crop went to feed people and livestock, many in undeveloped countries." Less than 5 percent of the corn supply in 2000 went into ethanol production. Thirteen years later, the 2013 harvest saw a more drastic result of 40 percent going into ethanol production, "45% was used to feed livestock, and only 15% was used for food and beverage."[3]

The more environmental pressure there is to produce biofuel from ethanol, the less corn the United States ships to the other nations of the world. And considering that many economies are dependent upon affordable food for their government's stability, that means less corn being shipped to the underdeveloped countries could lead their populations to become more desperate for basic survival. This in turn will cause more diplomatic unrest, perhaps leading to more revolutions and a greater vacuum for power in regions such as the Middle East.

I know it takes a little bit of thinking to grasp how a cornfield in Iowa and an Arab spring in Egypt are connected, but when you consider how intricately woven together the nations of the world are today, it's not too far of a stretch.

The greenest thing about the environmental issue is the money that can be gained by it. Several other crops and grasses can be used for biofuel production, but corn is the one that was initially incentivized by tax credits, and the process of planting, harvesting, and producing the by-product is already in place. If the issue were truly what's best for the environment, then corn would be used to feed people and some other resource used for fuel. But since the real issue is power and who's in control, governments claim that we must promote ethanol or we will destroy the world we are leaving for our children.

It's one of the clearest examples in our time of how, under the banner of fighting global warming, environmentalism is being used to control people.

THE CONTINUING RELEVANCE OF OIL

Today, if you claim that climate change is a myth, you are blasted with names like "Moron!" and "Fool!" On the other hand, if you make the case that this is one of the greatest threats in our world, you are applauded and considered courageous and groundbreaking. The pressure to conform is immense.

The United States first observed Earth Day in 1970, and since that time, climate change has become a polarizing issue. The University of Texas's latest UT Energy Poll found that more than nine out of ten survey respondents (91 percent) under age thirty-five say climate change is occurring, compared with 74 percent of those age sixty-five or older.[4] Could it be that the younger generation was raised in classrooms with textbooks dedicated to the topics of climate change, global warming, ozone depletion, and greenhouse gas emissions?

While the United States is using tax dollars to subsidize "green energy" to combat the perceived threat of climate change, other nations of the world are thumbing their noses at the idea and remain in pursuit of oil. Oil is the major economic reason that the Middle East is such a global focal point. The Middle East has a lot of it, and the world still needs it, regardless of what some may say.

As for my own country, we have deliberately let this situation develop. No oil refinery has been built inside the United States since 1976 because of environmentalist concerns. While the United States has the ability to become energy independent by drilling here at home and pumping our own oil, we don't have the ability to refine and produce the volume of fuel we would need because of the environmental choke hold we have put on the energy sector.

Meanwhile, what are the Russians doing? Are they looking for ways to convert algae into biodiesel? No! They are looking for a way to reestablish the military might of the former Soviet Union. They are moving across the Ukraine and the Crimean Peninsula. They are willing to use their military strength and resources in Syria and other parts of the Middle East to assist the enemies of Israel in order to secure more oil.

Russia is already a major petroleum producer, so they do not need more oil for themselves. But if they can control the oil reserves of the world, then they can set the price at a level that transfers the wealth of the world into their pockets. Once that occurs, Russia's desire not only to return to the status of a world superpower, but to be the *only* superpower, will be a reality. Remember, "He who has the gold makes the rules."

Why else would Russia be taking an advisory role with Iran (whose sworn purpose, it happens, is to destroy Israel and the West)? They want what Iran has: oil and access to more oil in the Middle East. And Russia has what Iran needs to accomplish its evil mission: nuclear weapons.

When issues like this are discussed, many people disregard the information as untrue, right-wing conspiracy talk, propaganda. There are several reasons for this type of thinking. Some don't want to believe that evil agendas like this exist in the world. But unfortunately they do. Others have bought in to the idea that the enemies of freedom and democracy around the world are misunderstood and oppressed and simply need an opportunity to experience the benefits of equality in order to live in peace. I assure you, raising the minimum wage at McDonald's is not going to change the agenda of terrorist and terror-supporting nations who believe what they believe as a matter of a demented doctrine.

Another reason this global agenda continues to gain traction in the West is the fact that Middle Eastern professors are teaching in the classrooms of many colleges and universities all across America. They have been funded by dollars that come to the institutions by way of the oil-producing nations of the Middle East. So it becomes easy to see why the Millennials graduating from America's schools care more about the environment and the global agenda than they do about freedom and about our only ally and the only democracy in the Middle East—the nation of Israel.

HOOKED

We've discussed Daniel and what he had to say about the end times. We've established that Jesus Christ told in great detail all that would take place before His return. Now I want to turn your attention back to Ezekiel, who told how a Russian and Islamic coalition was going to form and orchestrate an invasion. What would cause such a coalition? For the radical Islamic faction, it would be a deep-seated hatred that goes all the way back to Isaac and Jacob. For the Russians, it's all about oil and a desire to control the world!

That is why we read the words "I will turn you around, put hooks into your jaws, and lead you out" in Ezekiel 38:4. The "hooks" are a reference to oil.

What is it about a hook that is significant? Picture an angler with a hook in the jaw of the fish he wants to catch. The fish may not want to come out of the water, but with a hook in its jaw, it has no choice but to go wherever it is pulled. In this illustration God is letting Ezekiel know that He is the one who is pulling the coalition into the conflict. The reason is to demonstrate in front of the entire world that "He who keeps Israel shall neither slumber nor sleep" (Psalm 121:4).

While the global thirst for oil increases, the topic is considered too environmentally unfriendly for the politically correct culture of the United States. Each player's attitudes are key components for the events that are about to unfold. The results will be felt in two areas. The first is the continued weakening of the U.S. economy. The second is an inability to engage in a major military action in a foreign theater.

In 2001 the United States engaged in the global "war on terror." Then-President Bush made it clear that this was not going to be a quick or easy conflict. In the years that have followed, the American people have grown war weary. Our flags seem to spend as much time at half-mast as they do full flight. We have learned that our enemies are willing to do whatever it takes to see their global agenda of terror and Islamic jihad carried out. Under the Obama administration, passive and weak foreign policy created a vacuum that was filled by Islamic terror states who feel empowered by America's softening.

Now it will require more strength and effort to once again stabilize a hostile and volatile region of the globe. The question is, will the American people have the stamina and strength to do it all again with another generation of service members facing the danger of IEDs and sleeper cells? And will the American economy have enough resources to support it? Even with a new leader in the White House who has identified the danger that radical Islam represents to the world, the writing is on the wall. Our enemies will not go down without a fight.

You may not have considered the environment to be a factor in the apocalypse until now, but I assure you it all goes together. Each aspect of what you see happening in the world today is a thread that is being woven into a tapestry that depicts the picture told by prophets centuries ago. The picture announces that the One who created the heavens and the earth is the One who was, and is, and—very soon—is to come.

TAKING THE MARK OF THE BEAST

He causes all, both small and great, rich and poor, free and slave,
to receive a mark on their right hand or on their foreheads,
and that no one may buy or sell except one who has the mark
or the name of the beast, or the number of his name.

—Revelation 13:16–17

In the previous two chapters, we listed a few of the many reasons why the world's current state of financial stress is the perfect setting for the type of global economic collapse that will give the Antichrist a platform. The world's economies are becoming more and more interrelated, with debt enslaving nations to other nations. Meanwhile, environmental extremism is weakening the United States and its allies even as it empowers overseas enemies.

Now, with Revelation 13, we come to a section of Scripture that has often caused people to pause and wonder, *Who would ever take the mark of the beast?* The "beast" mentioned in Revelation 13 is the same as the "little horn" of Daniel 7. He is the Antichrist. We're not exactly sure what the "mark" is going to be like, but it is clearly some kind of identification that permits a person to participate in the new economy that the Antichrist will rule over.

In less technological times, it must have puzzled people how such an identification system could even be possible. For us, we might wonder why anyone would submit to such an intrusive ID method. And yet the deeper we dig into the challenges that we face in the world today, the more likely it appears that people will line up by the masses for the opportunity.

A Craving for Identity Security

Think about the demand we have right now for foolproof identification methods. It's come to the forefront with the rise in identity theft.

Identity theft is one of the fastest-growing crimes in the world today. For certain, there have long been dishonest people who have forged someone's checks or had a fake ID card, but the more technology has become common in everyday life, the more people are being impacted by this problem. It is estimated that each year around eighteen million Americans are victims of identity theft in some way. The estimated annual cost of identity theft is fifteen billion dollars.[1] We've all watched the media cover how often computer servers with thousands of names, filled with mountains of private information, have been hacked and the data compromised.

Earlier I mentioned the events of 9/11. Following that horrific tragedy, the 9/11 Commission Report analyzed and outlined what went wrong. Within the pages of the report is a section of about ten pages that details potential solutions for identity theft. Why? Because terrorists use identity theft as a means of being able to move from place to place without getting caught.[2]

We have no-fly lists, but all that needs to be done to circumvent them is for someone to steal another person's name and modify his appearance, and suddenly he becomes someone else. In the hypersensitive, politically correct Western culture, however, we would rather vilify and harass an agent who dares to profile a suspicious person than allow the agent to take a second look at someone who fits the bill. This is even after law enforcement officials and national security experts have pointed out that in the al-Qaeda training manuals the terrorist trainees are told to leave their camp with no fewer than five fake IDs. Another section even instructs them on how to live off credit card fraud while hiding in the United States.[3]

We know we need more comprehensive and effective security methods. At least as recently as 2014, security analysts for identity protection companies have said that it is time to retire the tried, true, and dearly coveted Social Security number, replacing it with something more effective for identification.[4]

The Social Security number goes back to December 1, 1936—the day John D. Sweeney Jr. was issued the very first number in New Rochelle, New York. It was originally issued to track tax contributions to the then-brand-new national retirement fund. But in the last eighty years, the Social Security number has become a much more common way to track identity than any other piece of data in the United States. It's used for student ID on college and university campuses. It's the number that banks assign to a customer. It is how large companies keep up with their employees. This one number was never intended to serve so many purposes, even to the point that in 1946 the cards themselves were printed with the words "Not For Identification." Yet the more consistently they are used to register at hospitals, take college entrance exams, and sign up for health care and insurance, the more identity theft will continue to be on the rise.

Social Security numbers and other common forms of identification all have problems, and with the rise in identity theft comes the growth in the risk it brings, not just to our economy but to our very lives.

STRANGER DANGER

Right now tens of thousands of people from the war-torn Middle East are seeking asylum in the West. In fiscal year 2016, the United States admitted approximately 39,000 Muslims who sought refugee status.[5] These individuals came through the channels of the State Department and have visas and permission to be here. One can only have compassion for those who have endured horrors and have had to flee their homelands. Yet others may come with different motives and bring risk with them.

President Obama, in his last days in office, entered into an agreement with the prime minister of Australia to bring into the United States the "refugees" that he refused to allow into his nation.[6] The Australian leader had refused to allow them into Australia because there was no way to validate who was a friend in need of help and asylum and who was a wolf in sheep's clothing. And that's the problem.

There isn't any reliable way to verify the data that those who claim to be refugees give about who they are or where they come from. All we really have to go by is their word. There are also troubling reports about the disproportionate number of young men who are seeking refuge in Europe and the West.[7]

While the circumstances of their situations are well documented by the media, as we see in war-torn Syria and in the atrocities committed by ISIS in Iraq and northern Africa, the one thing that is not well documented is the real purpose of those who want to come to the United States.

Because the surge in immigration is so great and our government does not possess the ability to gather the relevant data quickly enough, many have called for a moratorium on immigration—to simply stop bringing foreigners into the country until we can catch up with who is here legally and who is breaking the law. Needless to say, the topic is controversial on all fronts. To take a side causes the kind of backlash and rancor that brands one a bigot by the left or a coward by the right. My purpose is not to persuade you in one direction or the other. I do, however, want you to see how these small matters (as they would seem) play into a much larger issue of social vulnerability that will cause the Antichrist to become a popular figure on the earth.

LIBERTY FORFEITED

Problem one: identity theft has a grave impact on the economy. Problem two: radical Islamic terrorists use this very vehicle to enter the country, and their stated purpose is to bring the United States and other "infidel" nations to their knees. Problem three: the society we live in, as a whole, doesn't know how to take care of itself and doesn't demonstrate a great desire to learn.

This is where the topic takes a twist. Bear with me for a moment while I approach the issue from another, more personal angle, and see if you can understand how this could lead individuals to willingly take the mark of the beast.

My grandparents on my father's side were born in 1911 and 1913. They grew up in a tough time and were tougher people because of it. They lived in an America where not every child born was expected to reach adulthood. As a matter of fact, my grandfather was one of ten children, and only he and five of his siblings survived to the age of eight.

His parents buried four children during the Spanish flu pandemic of 1918–20. They were not people of much financial means and so they learned to survive off the land where they lived. Most of what they ate, they grew in a garden, raised in the pasture, or harvested from the field. When I came along in 1978, they lived in what they considered the city, and yet they still had a garden in the yard with rows of vegetables, cans of pickled peppers on the shelf in the pantry, and a freezer full of meat that would last until the next fishing trip.

The point is, they were self-sufficient for their basic needs. The idea that a world leader was going to force people from their generation to take a mark on their hand or forehead in order to buy or sell was out of the question. They could grow their own food. They knew what it took to survive. They were not afraid of hard times; they had lived through them before and were willing to endure them again if it meant the opportunity to remain free. They valued liberty more than they did comfort and convenience.

Few people today are like them. In fact, my grandparents' values are hard for many today to even comprehend. We're more comfortable, but we're also more compliant. We look for others to take care of us. And we don't necessarily have the discernment to see what our would-be providers are really like.

So who will take the mark of the beast? People who live in an age when a universal ID system is technologically possible, people who think such a system is needed to keep their finances and their lives safe, and people who have become overly trusting of authority figures.

AS IT WAS BEFORE THE FLOOD

Of that day and hour no one knows, not even the angels of heaven,
but My Father only. But as the days of Noah were,
so also will the coming of the Son of Man be.

—Matthew 24:36–37

We've seen how the Antichrist is going to come to power through a global economic crisis. Now we are going to pull the veil back on the type of culture the Bible describes as prevailing in the end times, further proving that the time of the coming of the Son of Man is near at hand.

I know, however, that every time this kind of conversation begins, certain individuals want to run to the verse above and misapply what it says. They want to broad-brush the issue by simply saying, "No one knows!"

It's true that no one knows exactly when the Lord Jesus will return. The verse clearly says that. But it also says that God the Father has kept this information to Himself. He knows. And it says we should look for a pattern of behavior ("as the days of Noah were") that will mark the approximate time.

When my wife and I were expecting our first child, we were aware that there was an expected day of delivery, and we even had a twenty-four-hour window marked off on the calendar when the doctor antici-pated that our daughter would be born. While I was excited and filled with expectation to meet our baby girl, I really didn't get jumpy about phone calls from my wife, nor was I constantly checking on her, until I knew we were close. When the last trimester began, the uncomfortable sighs from my wife expressed the fact that she was in need of relief . . . and soon!

There were more than enough people offering free advice about what we should watch for or telling us what had happened to them.

"You never know with the first one!" some well-meaning church lady would say.

"I carried like you, and mine was a month early," the next mom we ran into would tell my wife.

"I had the same craving. My son was three weeks overdue," another woman would say.

If my wife and I had believed all the unsolicited information we got when we were expecting our first child, we would have lost our minds many times over before our child was born. But while neither of us had any way of knowing the exact time she would enter the world—for the record, 3:02 p.m. on April 16, 2005—we did know by certain undeni-able signs that we were getting really close in the days leading up to her arrival.

The point is, we can look at the culture we are living in and see undeniable signs that we are close to the Lord's arrival. I am going to point out a few. See what you think.

LOVE GROWN COLD

Jesus said, "As the days of Noah were, so also will the coming of the Son of Man be." So what were the days of Noah like? We know pretty clearly from Genesis 6:5: "The LORD saw that the wickedness of man was great in the earth, and that every intent of the thoughts of his heart was only evil continually." These were days when everyone did what they wanted without worrying about the consequences.

Now, what are the days that we live in like? Look around you, and you see individuals doing as they please without any concern for the consequences.

In an earlier verse, Jesus said it this way: "Because lawlessness will abound, the love of many will grow cold" (Matthew 24:12). Notice two words used one right after the other—"lawlessness" and "abound." It is not going to be a minor cropping up of bad behavior; it is going to be a widespread pattern, and it will impact the attitude of believers. That's why Christ said their love would grow cold.

I have spent my fair share of time discussing the world's problems with people who would like to help solve them. I've heard folks talk about everything from the homeless and the hungry, to evangelism on school campuses, to orphanages and rehabilitation centers for those who need another chance at life. And it seems like, more often than not, for all they say they want to do and all they feel inspired to achieve, they discard the idea with the words, "What good would it do anyway?" They look at the size of the problem they are trying to solve and feel as though it is much greater than they have the ability to manage. So why should they try?

That attitude is a fulfillment of the words that Jesus Christ gave to His disciples. Their love has grown cold.

Consider some other passages of Scripture to define the kind of love that Jesus is talking about in this verse.

On one occasion Christ was asked by a young lawyer, "What shall I do to inherit eternal life?" (Luke 10:25). Now, the eternal life the young man was referring to is the reward of life in heaven. Remember, everyone will spend eternity somewhere. The question is, where?

In the conversation and debate that follows, the word "love" becomes a key component to eternal reward. " 'You shall love the LORD your God with all your heart, with all your soul, with all your strength, and with all your mind,' and 'your neighbor as yourself' " (Luke 10:27). The message is clear. Love is not what you say; love is what you do. Love is an action that does not need to be explained, because when others see you demonstrating the behavior of love, they will know beyond a doubt where your affections lie.

When someone notices a person waxing his sports car with a soft cloth until he can see the reflection of his face glowing back at him, there is no doubt that he loves the car. When someone notices the same person neglect the emotional needs of the family inside the home where the car is parked, he or she may say that he loves them but he doesn't demonstrate it. That's why the verse contains the quote that says we should love our neighbor as ourselves. Until you demonstrate love, it's only a feeling and not a fact. While in the last section we discussed the currency of the world being money, it is obvious that the currency of heaven is love.

I won't go too much further down the road on this topic, but let me point out that Christ was telling us one of the things to look for as an indicator of the coming day was that believers would stop acting like believers. They wouldn't show the kind of love that would let others know what they cared about. Their love would grow cold and dormant. It would be there, but it would be inactive.

What's the Big Deal?

Have you noticed how outspoken our generation is about the things we care about? I am surprised at how committed people can be to the things that move them. They will proclaim their attachment on any platform available, invite others to become a part of it, and invest their time, money, and thought into becoming better at it. They will stay informed about the latest developments and make sure that if anything is updated they are able to acquire it, and then celebrate the success or lament the failures. The list of potential causes or topics that generate such passion is endless.

Today people love hobbies. They love sports. They love technology. They love causes. They love groups of people who love what they love, and they are not ashamed to show it. They travel in packs and keep up with each other on social media. They look out for each other and hold one another accountable so that they achieve success. "I haven't seen you at the gym class lately!" If it's a sports team, you wear their colors. If it's a marathon, you buy a sticker to let everyone know how far you ran. If it's cycling, you have a sign that says, "Share the road." If it's a pet, you post its likeness with an "I (heart) my labradoodle" caption. On and on it goes.

The world we live in is not ashamed to love anything and everything out loud and in the open. But when it comes to the area of our faith, we draw back in the concern that we might offend someone.

I assure you, allowing our love to grow cold is offensive to the God who sent His Son to pay for our redemption with His very life. So why do people do it? According to Matthew 24:12, it's the abundance of "lawlessness." Back in Noah's day, people did as they pleased and it seemed as though they never suffered a single consequence. No wrath was poured out; no one was stricken with a plague; no one wore a scarlet letter. So they just did as they wished. It was socially acceptable and no one seemed to mind. Similarly, in our generation, the consequences of lawlessness are neither immediate nor extreme, so the attitude is, *What's the big deal?*

The big deal is, there is a payday someday.

In my younger days, I was often asked what I thought my father might do "if." In other words, if I said a certain word, if I misbehaved and got sent to the principal's office, if I broke curfew on the weekend, it was as though they believed that, because he was Pastor Hagee, the punishment would be severe! For the record, my father was and is a very fair and loving man, but when it came to discipline and consequence for breaking the rules, I didn't ever have to wonder about the If Factor. I knew.

The way I knew was that I had an older brother who took all of the guesswork out of the question of "if" for me. He was six years older than I was, and by the time I got to the age where being mischievous was attractive, I didn't have to guess what the consequences would be. I was aware of how justice at the Hagee house would be administered if I stepped over the line. That doesn't mean I lived the perfect life of a saint, but it does mean I wasn't surprised when I learned about the consequences that would come with my behavior.

Carefully read again what is written to us about the end times and the days of Noah. Just as the people in Noah's day "did not know until the flood came and took them all away, so also will the coming of the Son of Man be" (Matthew 24:39). There's your example. They watched Noah build his ark for 120 years. They heard the daily pounding of the nails. They mocked him for the idea that the vessel would ever set float on the waves. Some laughed when they saw the way the animals came and entered the floating sanctuary. Others paused for a moment to consider what they saw and then just went along as though it meant nothing. Then Noah got on board with his family and God closed the door (see Genesis 7:16). Those who were inside were safe and those on the outside were doomed. It was too late.

The message to us in this generation should be perfectly clear. There is a "flood" coming, a judgment of God, just as it came in Noah's day. The example has been set and history is repeating itself. Like Noah, who was called "a preacher of righteousness" (2 Peter 2:5), pastors and faithful teachers have taught for centuries about the coming of the Lord. Even though we see the world racing in every conceivable way toward the moment, people still want to behave as if it will not occur. It will. And the very fact that they are acting as deniers of the faith rather than as believers is evidence that we are closer than you think.

IT'S ALL ABOUT ME

Know this, that in the last days perilous times
will come: For men will be lovers of themselves,
lovers of money, boasters, proud, blasphemers,
disobedient to parents, unthankful, unholy,
unloving, unforgiving, slanderers, without
self-control, brutal, despisers of good, traitors,
headstrong, haughty, lovers of pleasure rather
than lovers of God, having a form of godliness
but denying its power.

—2 Timothy 3:1–5

When Paul was telling Timothy about conditions that will prevail in the last days, the first quality he mentioned was excessive self-love. "For men will be lovers of themselves . . ." With that in mind, can there be any doubt that the times the prophets spoke of are indeed here?

We live in a time when the world is all about the individual. We have coined terms such as *me time, self-help,* and *selfie.* While these may seem like minor cultural fads, they have a significant role in telling us where we are in Bible prophecy and what's going to happen next.

It hasn't always been like this.

MORAL PARAGON OR DEBASED HYPOCRITE?

In July 2014, I took my children to Washington, DC, to introduce them to the rich history of our nation and help them better understand what it means to be an American. We took a day excursion to tour Mount Vernon, the historic home of George Washington, located just outside the Beltway in the Virginia countryside.

As a child, I had heard an evolving history on George Washington. When I was small, it was about a young boy with an ax and a cherry tree who could not tell a lie. As I entered my senior year of high school and began basic history requirements at the university, I heard words such as *deist* and *greedy* and *desperate* applied to Washington. Sometimes it's difficult to know what you should believe—the portrait of a dignified general kneeling in prayer, asking God for mercy at Valley Forge, or the modern version of a bigoted greedmonger desperate for power and willing to do almost anything to get it. One version tells the story of honor, duty, and sacrifice; the other fits the narrative that the United States has been wrong from the start.

I am glad I took my children to Mount Vernon that day, because it was only by seeing with my own eyes that I could draw my personal conclusion.

We entered the property through large iron gates leading to a circular drive. We then bought our tickets and walked into the welcome center, which led up a hill to the historic residence. I was immediately overcome by a feeling that every room had a story and that every inch of the five hundred acres was important. The place exuded a solemn presence of history.

I learned several things about the Washington family, the property they managed, and the risks they took when they decided to stand up to the British crown and fight for independence.

First, it's important to note that Mount Vernon is located on land Washington's great-grandfather claimed in 1674. By 1730, the property had grown to more than eight thousand acres that were mainly used for agriculture, the export-import industry, and trade.

George Washington did much more than plow and plant on his farm; he was a natural entrepreneur. In fact, he had several enterprises on the property that were quite successful. Washington found a way to capture the natural resources of the Potomac River and made the first-ever fishery, where he could pack the fish in salt and ship them to Europe. He produced corn, wheat, tobacco, beef, pork, lamb, and wool and raised horses. He sent his goods around the world because his property accessed the Potomac, which led to the Atlantic. He was one of the most successful private landowners and businessmen in the world before the American Revolution.

Why is this important to know? Because if one of your current beliefs about Washington is that he was greedy, then the fact that he was already doing very well financially before the Revolution seems to be strong evidence against that myth.

Second, the property housed a chapel where regular church services were held. The tour fully documented how sacred the Word of God was to the Washington family, especially for its patriarch. So if the founder of our nation was "godless," as some have suggested, then why would he make such a statement about his faith in his personal life?

By the end of the day, I had a totally different view of George Washington and a great appreciation for what he was willing to risk in order to establish my opportunity to live in a free country.

His success in business was primarily made possible through shipping, so as soon as the Revolutionary War began, the British Navy enforced a strict blockade that directly affected Washington's export business. He was a man of deep personal conviction and faith, and the Revolution was important enough to him that he spoke about it publicly.

The bottom line: Washington wasn't selfish; he was sacrificial. He didn't fit the description Paul wrote about in 2 Timothy. He didn't love himself or money more than he did the conviction of being free. He wasn't blasphemous or unthankful. He wasn't a despiser of good, nor a lover of self rather than of God. I wasn't at Valley Forge in the winter of 1777–78, and I am quite certain neither were any of the historians who are on the earth today. What I can tell you is that what I experienced firsthand at Mount Vernon that day fits more with the character of the man I saw kneeling in a portrait than what some these days want to report as "fact."

Washington is just one example of how far we've shifted from a lifestyle of service and sacrifice to an attitude of selfishness.

Until recently, sacrifice for others was a deeper conviction than love of self. President Kennedy said it with great candor at his inaugural address: "Ask not what your country can do for you—ask what you can do for your country."[1] Now, you may read these words and dismiss them as a political sound bite. But weigh their truth against the reality of the world we live in today and see if they are not much more than that.

Ask yourself not . . .

- what the government can do for you.
- what your company can do for you.
- what your family can do for you.

- what your church can do for you.

But ask . . .

- what you can do for them.

How can you make others stronger? What gifts and talents have you been given that will help others reach their goals, not just help you pursue your own?

If George Washington had had a modern mind-set in 1776, there would be no United States of America today. Why? Because there was too much at stake. Too much business would be lost. Property could be confiscated. All he had worked for would vanish. But instead he thought about generations of people he would never meet, and he knew that if he didn't do something, then they would never be free.

The Many Dismal Expressions of Self-Centeredness

I hope, indeed, that you possess a character more in line with the father of the American nation. If you do, though, that means you are out of step with the trend of today's culture. Here are some hard facts and plain observations that tell the story.

Inattention to Others

These days we would rather sit and text on a phone than talk to the people who are sitting across from us. We believe that what we have to say to someone else at a distance is more important than connecting with the individuals who are within reach.

Could you imagine if you sat at a table to eat a meal with someone who brought a typewriter? As you ask him questions, he looks down at the page and punches away on the keys. No matter how much of your soul and secrets you pour out, he just nods and says,

"Right" or "Absolutely" or maybe even "I totally agree." But you know he's focused on the typewriter and that he really isn't listening. *Ding, crank.* He shoves the platen back to the left and taps out another sentence. Can you imagine that? You'd feel as though you didn't mean much to him and that he would rather be somewhere else.

I doubt anyone has experienced the scene I just described exactly as it's written, but the next time you are in a restaurant, look around the room and notice how many people are ignoring each other and typing away on their phones. This is the kind of thing that happens when people are "lovers of themselves" (2 Timothy 3:2).

Boastfulness

Another sign that we are living in perilous times is that we are "boasters" (2 Timothy 3:2).

Listen to a postgame interview. The franchise player will talk about himself in the third person. He will fill the air with what he did and how he felt unappreciated when he did it, and how it's hard to be who he is, with all the pressure that's on him to perform.

Now, I'm not purposely singling out professional athletes, because I personally have met several who don't fit this description. But there are many we have seen and heard who do, and plenty of nonathletes who do the same!

Disobedience to Authority

Another sign is that we have a generation that is terribly "disobedient to parents" (2 Timothy 3:2). I find it ironic that Paul wrote this description two thousand years ago, and yet such disobedience is everywhere in our culture today.

When I was a child, anyone taller than me rated an automatic "Yes sir" or "Yes ma'am." The idea that I would respond to an adult with a "Huh?" or a "What?" was out of the question. Doing what I was told to do by my parents was not rewarded with special praise; it was expected behavior because I was taught as a child to obey. By being taught to show proper respect to authority, I knew how to adhere to structure as an adult.

Recently, we've watched entire sections of cities burn because of uncontrolled rage. As communities sought to express their understandable anguish over tragic situations, certain factions inflamed crowds to respond with destruction and more tragedy, instead of taking steps that lead to change. We have seen years' worth of work and care literally go up in smoke as stores are torched and looters take what they want. And the people who have nothing to do with causing the problem are devastated by the mobs that, in Paul's words, are "without self-control, brutal, despisers of good" (2 Timothy 3:3).

When trouble began in Ferguson, Missouri, and Baltimore, Maryland, the leaders in the city of San Antonio got together to discuss what could be done to prevent such behavior from taking place in our city. Business leaders spoke; the mayor and the city council members said a few words; pastors got up and offered their prayers. But the one statement that echoed in my spirit that day came from the assistant chief of the police force. He looked at pastors and other city leaders gathered and said, "Please teach your children from an early age to be polite to others, say 'Please' and 'Thank you,' 'Yes sir' and 'yes ma'am.' If you will teach them to respect authority when they are young, they will not disrespect us when they are older."[2]

I thought, *We've done it to ourselves.* In an effort to obtain more, we have forgotten what is most important. We have neglected to teach the basics of what it means to be kind to one another. Here we sat in a room, talking about sophisticated programs that we hoped would make a difference, when the answer was simply to get back to the basics of instructing our children how to be well behaved.

FROM SELF-DENYING TO SELF-SEEKING

While you could certainly find examples of selfishness in past generations, in this generation we've got Paul's description nailed down to the last letter: "Lovers of pleasure rather than lovers of God, having a form of godliness but denying its power" (2 Timothy 3:4–5). This tells us that the problem of selfishness has made deep inroads into the church. The problem is not just with *them*—the unbelievers. It's also with *us*. We who call ourselves by the name of Christ reveal who we really care about the most when it comes down to whose interests we are concerned about the most—our own or God's.

We live in a generation that has more access to church than any other. We can go to a service that is exciting, dynamic, and filled with more talent than any major production in town. We can watch church on network television or the Internet. We have bookstores filled with resources and conferences of every type. And yet for all we have access to, is it making us any better?

The Bible describes the early church by saying, "They did not love their lives to the death" (Revelation 12:11). In other words, they loved the Lord more than their own lives. That doesn't fit with the modern church of the West. In our modern culture, the church is busy creating a doctrine that makes us comfortable rather than compelling us to change, and in doing so we have thrown out the discipline of our faith and adopted an attitude of self-justification. We want to feel good without being good, rather than hear the Word and do it.

Christ put it this way: "If anyone desires to come after Me, let him deny himself" (Luke 9:23). In a generation that is totally absorbed with self, these are hard words to hear.

FACING THE TRUTH

I mentioned at the beginning of this book that my purpose was to tell you the truth, by using scriptures in the unveiling of what is to come. It may not always be easy to embrace the Word of God, but it is always accurate. One truth is this: "in the last days perilous times will come" (2 Timothy 3:1). They are unavoidable because "men will be lovers of themselves" (verse 2).

Stop and consider the world we live in today and ask yourself, *Is there any question as to whether or not we are in the last days?* The answer is clear.

HIGH-DEF APOCALYPSE

You, Daniel, shut up the words, and seal the book until the time of the end; many shall run to and fro, and knowledge shall increase.

—Daniel 12:4

wasn't alive when Neil Armstrong walked on the moon and spoke the often-quoted words, "One small step for man, one giant leap for mankind." But if I could take the liberty, I would add, "And one huge sign for those who study prophecy!"

My father was attending Trinity University and was in the campus library the day Commander Armstrong captured the attention of the world as he planted the American flag on the moon. My father stood there with other students watching a television in wonder while an older man from the custodial staff was tending to his job across the room. History was being made and broadcast to the world before his eyes, but he simply shook his head and said, "It can't be so. It just can't be so."

That's how fast things are changing in our time. Technology is moving so quickly that one generation can't believe it, another is amazed by it, and a third shrugs their shoulders and asks, "What next?" And all this change is another cultural reality telling us that we're living at the end of days.

A NEW WORLD

When Daniel received his revelation of the apocalypse and the things to come, he was told by God to seal up his book, because the words would not be completely fulfilled until "many shall run to and fro, and knowledge shall increase" (12:4). Daniel was talking about a time when there would be much more travel and vastly increased quantities of information. He probably couldn't imagine what that would really be like or when it would come about, yet isn't that what we see in modern technological times?

In addition to man walking on the moon, let me give you some more examples.

Travel

When my grandmother's family moved to East Texas, her father loaded her and seven siblings into a covered wagon pulled by two gray mules to make the trip. She traveled as a child much like Mary did on her way from Galilee to Bethlehem nearly two thousand years before. I use the comparison, not to say that my grandmother's move as a child was a holy pilgrimage like Mary and Joseph's, but to point out that for millennia not much changed in this world with regard to travel. Abraham rode on horses and used livestock to pull his conveyance. Fourteen generations later, King David did the same. Twenty-eight generations later, so did people traveling in Christ's time. And by the early 1900s, many were still doing the same thing.

Then—the possibilities exploded! Just think of what has been accomplished in the last 125 years in travel alone. Automobiles. Submarines. Air travel. National and private space travel. Hyperloop trains.

The progress in the means and speed of travel is staggering, and it shows no signs of stopping.

It used to take several days, weeks, or even months to get where you were going. Now you can be on the other side of the world in a matter of hours. Running to and fro indeed.

Communication

When my father was a child in the 1940s, his house phone was on a party line. To be connected, you had to get hold of an operator by turning a handle on the side of the receiver box. Then you would have to wait till the operator could connect you, and the number of houses on the phone line determined the number of rings that needed to occur for you to know that a call was intended for you. For example, if you were the first house on the party line, you would hear a brief single *ring*. If you were the second house, it was *ring, ring*. The third house, three short rings. And so on.

Making a long-distance call was a complicated task. While my father and his family lived between Beaumont and Houston, his grandparents lived in Coolidge, Arizona. If my grandfather wanted to talk to his mother, he would call the operator in Houston and ask to be connected to the operator in Arizona. Then he would have to wait for a line to become available, and she would plug him in to the line that connected him to Arizona. Once talking to the operator in Arizona, he would then give that operator the information needed for his mother's home phone, and the operator would tell him to wait by the line while they made contact with her and then they would call him back. Often it took longer to connect the call than it did for the conversation to take place.

Now, with wireless technology, you don't even have to dial the number. If you have the contact name stored in your phone, you just push a button, and it will connect you to any number on any continent that receives a cell signal. That's how far communication has come in the last seventy-five years.

Connectedness

When I was a child, about the only thing you could do to entertain yourself in the car was sing songs with never-ending verses or play the "quiet game" (my parents' favorite). Now my children sit in peaceful silence wearing headsets and watching anything they can access on streaming devices.

When I was a freshman at the Oral Roberts University School of Business in 1996, my communications course included a chapter on how to use a typewriter for business purposes. I remember my elderly professor talking about how she couldn't see how electronic mail would ever take the place of a well-written business letter. By the time I graduated, she had retired and we had to go back through the course to learn how to use the computer for e-mail.

Back in those days, if you had a cell phone on my college campus, it looked like a radio issued by the army with an antenna long enough to call in an airstrike. A text message was too cumbersome to send because you had to punch through way too many symbols and options before you could get to the letter you wanted. Now a text message is more common than a handshake, and the U.S. Postal Service is trying to survive because no one is licking stamps anymore.

Technology has enabled us to access more information than we could have ever dreamed of. It may not make us smarter, but it does connect us more quickly.

Medical Care

Consider, too, the advancements in the area of medicine. Fifty years ago in the United States, if you were past the age of seventy-five, you were 1 in 35,000. If you were eighty-five, you were 1 in 250,000. If you were past ninety-five, you were 1 in 500,000. Now there are more than 450,000 people around the world who are one hundred years old or older.[1]

Our knowledge of nutrition and the adverse effects of unsafe habits, such as smoking, has increased. The array of available pharmaceuticals and the options for surgical procedures have vastly expanded. Vaccines and antibiotics have scored victories over infectious and parasitic diseases. All these and more have contributed to lengthening life spans.

There was a time when, once you stopped breathing, you were considered dead. Now, because of what science has achieved, we have redefined death. A machine can breathe for you; another can make your heart pump; another monitors your brain waves. Some people have to go to court and get a judge to write an order to turn off the machines that keep what would otherwise be a dead person alive.

Perhaps not all of the changes in medicine have been for the best. But undeniably, the growth in information and the advancement of technology have helped to make changes possible.

WHAT OUR TECH IS DOING TO US

The increase of knowledge has done a lot of wonderful things, but it has also created some areas of concern as well.

A Globalized Economy

Earlier, I discussed the economy and the perils that it is heading for. Technology plays a role in that. It would not be possible for the monies of the world to be nearly as connected as they are without technology. There was a time when such commodities would have been loaded on ships and sailed across the ocean. Now, with the push of a button, fortunes can be moved around the world instantaneously. As we've seen, technology is also one of the reasons identity theft has become an increasing problem.

Longer Lives and Greater Consumption

Many scientists believe that one of the reasons we are seeing a global warming trend is because there are more people living on the earth than at any other time.[2] This is due, in large part, to the advancements made in science and technology. Think about the statistics I listed earlier, including the fact that there are nearly 450,000 people at or over the age of one hundred alive today. That is roughly the same number of people who live in Washington, DC. Therefore, we are basically talking about an entire city whose population is one hundred years of age or older. They need to consume goods and services, which must be produced in factories, carried in trucks, and sold on shelves. I am definitely not trying to say that a person living longer is the problem, but it seems to me that scientists and governments are declaring that their continued consumption is contributing to the destruction of our planet's resources.

An Aging Society and the Economic Burden of Elder Care

Another economic problem attributed to technology is Social Security. The system was intended to be made available to one generation of Americans at the point when they would need it, on or about the same time that their predecessors would likely be dead and gone. Again, I certainly do not want to, in any way, cause you to think that I am saying the elderly are a burden. But let's consider what technology has done to the Baby Boom and succeeding generations.

About the time that knowledge really started to explode, so did birthing rates. During the Baby Boom, from 1945 to 1960, American families averaged 3.77 children per household.[3] This was a robust number because it meant there were enough children per house to produce an income that would help take care of two parents and two grandparents. Considering that in 1945 people seldom lived past the age of seventy-five, the economic model of Social Security seemed to work well.

Then science did some wonderful and terrible things. On one side, medical treatments got better and people lived longer. On the other side, the medical procedure of abortion has taken the lives of more than 58 million consumers, producers, and contributors out of the economic model in the United States alone.[4]

Now consider the fact that Generation X parents didn't match the birthing rate of the baby boomers. They used advancement in modern medicine in the form of birth control and then began producing fewer children per household.[5] Their children, the current Millennial generation, are following the pattern and showing even more reluctance to have kids.[6]

In just three generations, new medical innovation has given these successive groups the ability to keep born people alive longer and kill more unborn people in the womb. Meanwhile, technology itself has become so fascinating that apparently people are more interested in investing in new gadgets than in raising a large family. The fact that our society is aging and younger generations can no longer fulfill Social Security's promises to older generations is a sign of the imbalance that has developed due to infatuation with new technology.

A BLESSING OR A CURSE

I am making the point that information and technologies of all kinds are growing exponentially and changing all our lives. It's just what Daniel predicted, and it's a sign that we're living in the end times. Technology will undoubtedly help to enable the Antichrist to have his day.

But I need to insert a caution. The use of technology isn't all bad.

I am not one of those folks who talks about the evils of innovation. All by itself, innovation is amoral, not immoral. Technology has never demonstrated a prejudice, nor does it have a code of conduct. In fact, I believe that, in many ways, people of faith have stunted our ability to have an impact in society by speaking against the resources of technology rather than harnessing them.

I'll give you a case in point.

When my father was a child, many pastors in America stood in their pulpits shouting against the evils of television. They would say, "You can tell where the devil lives in your town because you can see his tail on the side of the roof!" This was referring to antennas, which were commonly used to get a signal on the TV set in the home. I've also heard some fiery old preachers talk about "the one-eyed demon squatting in the corner," referring to the "tube" sitting in families' living rooms waiting to be switched on. What they were saying about television was mostly ridiculous, and here's why.

When God told Daniel about an increase of knowledge, He wasn't in any way saying knowledge was evil. He was simply identifying what would be happening on the earth when the book would be reopened and the prophecies within it fulfilled.

I know some who behave as though, by avoiding technology, they are holding off the end times. Let's be perfectly clear. You could live as primitively as a caveman and you still would not move up or slow down by one nanosecond what God has ordered from the beginning of time.

I think it's sad that my grandfather's generation of preachers fought against the platform of media that has given my father's generation the opportunity to preach to the nations of the world. Literally hundreds of millions of people have heard the gospel because Christians and technology joined forces rather than waging war.

I sometimes wonder what would have happened if we had started sooner. Did you know there was a time when the media industry had a more open mind to ministries than it does today? There was a time when television networks ran out of content and many of them played the national anthem to close out the day's broadcast and then simply ran a test pattern until the next programming day began. What if during those early days the leaders of the church had embraced the technology? What if they had gone to the networks and told them that they would put their sermons on TV in the hours that the network didn't have anything else to show? Do you think we would be living in a different world than we are living in now?

Knowledge, innovation, and technology are not evil. They are fascinating but not demonic. Proverbs 9:10 says, "The fear of the LORD is the beginning of wisdom." The information is not wrong; it's the values of the society that accesses the information that is wrong.

What I can conclude though is we are living in a generation in which knowledge has increased and we now have the ability to watch the end draw nearer in high-def as we go!

THE ARSENAL OF THE FINAL CONFLICTS

This shall be the plague with which the LORD will strike
all the people who fought against Jerusalem:
Their flesh shall dissolve while they stand on their feet,
Their eyes shall dissolve in their sockets,
And their tongues shall dissolve in their mouths.

—Zechariah 14:12

I am a sixth-generation pastor. All of my life, I have heard members of my family discuss the Bible and try to determine where we are on God's prophetic clock. The conversations that my father had with his father are very different from the ones he and I have today.

For example, prior to 1948, it wasn't possible to understand what Isaiah said regarding a nation being born in a day (see Isaiah 66:8). On May 14, 1948, the mystery was solved. The nation born was Israel, and the prophecy was fulfilled.

Prior to 1967, my grandparents didn't know when "the times of the Gentiles are fulfilled" (Luke 21:24), because the city of Jerusalem wasn't yet in Jewish hands. But by the end of the Six-Day War, no one had to wonder anymore.

When my grandfather and his father read about a plague so intense that human beings would literally melt so fast that the skin on their bones would fall off before their bodies hit the ground, it was a major prophetic mystery. The public could not imagine what would create such a "plague" . . . until one summer morning in August of 1945.

The prophet Daniel spoke of knowledge increasing (see Daniel 12:4), and without question the growth of knowledge on how to build weapons of mass destruction is one of the most perilous developments of our age.

New and Most Cruel

As Hitler's war in Europe expanded, a number of American scientists, most of whom were refugees from fascist European countries, were concerned about the nuclear weapons research being conducted by Nazi Germany. So in 1940 the U.S. government made the decision to begin its own nuclear weapons program.[1]

The U.S. Army Corp of Engineers was given the task of building huge facilities for a top-secret mission code-named the Manhattan Project. For several years these scientists worked covertly in developing the key materials required for weapons-grade uranium and plutonium. Once the materials for the bomb were created, they were transported to Los Alamos, New Mexico, where another team assembled the materials into a functioning atomic bomb. This bomb was first tested in Alamogordo, New Mexico, on the morning of July 16, 1945, six weeks after Allied forces had defeated Nazi Germany.

The war in Europe had been long and bitter. America and her Western allies were ready for peace and eager to bring their battle-weary boys home. Germany engaged in many intense battles, from D-day to the Battle of the Bulge, and fought hard right up to the point of surrender. This same kind of determination to keep on resisting as long as possible was going to be the case with the Japanese in the Pacific, if not more so. The Japanese were willing to sacrifice all their soldiers, in spite of the fact that they had little chance of winning, because surrender meant you were a coward and therefore not worth the breath it took to keep you alive. So between April and mid-July of 1945, the Japanese had inflicted heavy casualties on the Allied forces. In fact, in that four-month period of intense fighting from island to island in the Pacific, more deaths occurred than in the previous three years of the war. This bloodbath proved that the Japanese were determined to take as many lives as they could even in the face of inevitable defeat.

General Douglas MacArthur was very much in favor of continuing the bombing and then following up with a ground invasion of Japan, much like the one that took place in the European campaign. But the early analysis of the invasion plan, named Operation Downfall, stated that such an invasion would cost up to one million American lives. That would be nearly ten times the number lost by all Allied forces in the D-day invasion. Quite possibly more than twice that number of Japanese, including civilians, would lose their lives in the extended conflict as well. The price was too high and an alternative was needed.

President Truman had been briefed on the test results of the A-bomb. He heard the misgivings of the Secretary of War, Supreme Allied Commander Dwight D. Eisenhower, and several of the scientists who worked on the project. They felt the weapon was immoral because of its ability to inflict massive death and destruction. But the president didn't want to lose any more American lives and believed the bomb would bring the war to a quick end.

On August 5, 1945, one of the B-29 Silverplate bombers was chosen as the strike plane for the first atomic attack mission on Japan. Code name: Operation Centerboard I. The aircraft would be flown by Lieutenant Colonel Paul W. Tibbets, commander of the 509th Composite Group. Lt. Col. Tibbets named the bomber *Enola Gay* after his mother, and just prior to the mission, her name was painted on the nose of the plane. The first atomic weapon ever used in the history of war was called Little Boy, and at 2:00 p.m. on the 5th of August, the bomb was loaded on a trailer and moved to the *Enola Gay*.

Five and half hours later, Lt. Col. Tibbets taxied the aircraft and began the twelve-hour mission. After making all of the required checkpoints while being escorted by several fighter planes, the *Enola Gay* at 0730 hours made its climb to thirty thousand feet. By 0750 hours, the shoreline of Japan was in its sights, and at 0830 hours a weather plane radioed the *Enola Gay* to say all was clear over the target.

At 0909 hours, for the first time since the mission began, Lt. Col. Tibbets informed the crew that the target was Hiroshima. The bombardier, Major Thomas Ferebee, took control of the plane, and at 0915 hours Little Boy was dropped. The drop took forty-three seconds, with the bomb falling to the ground a little faster than the speed of sound.

The explosion wiped out 90 percent of the city, instantly killing approximately eighty thousand people. Tens of thousands would later die from radiation exposure.

Three days later, a second B-29 dropped another A-bomb on Nagasaki, killing more than seventy thousand.[2]

Japan's Emperor Hirohito announced the country's unconditional surrender in a radio address on August 15, 1945, specifically saying the reason was "a new and most cruel bomb."[3] The war was finally over. Our boys were coming home. And the question regarding "the plague" described in Zechariah was finally answered.

PUTTING NUCLEAR WEAPONS IN THE HANDS OF ISRAEL'S ENEMIES

Now the possibility of nuclear war has come to the Middle East. While Zechariah says this is a plague that God will unleash on the enemies of Israel, it is America's own State Department that has decided to give this capability to the radical Islamic state of Iran. For nearly forty years, Iran and its high-ranking Shiite religious authority, the ayatollah, have been waging war with the United States. Anti-American and anti-Israeli sentiment has been at the heart of Iran's Islamic revolution even before the Beirut marine barracks bombing in 1983. Iran officially claimed no responsibility for the Beirut attack but then in 2004 erected a monument to commemorate bombings and its "martyrs."[4] The bottom line is, the radical Islamic state of Iran is not our friend and it supports some of our other enemies.

In July 2015, U.S. Secretary of State John Kerry signed an agreement with Iran that was unpopular in the United States and had many people concerned about the protections it offered to America and the rest of the world. Since the signing of the agreement, Iran has violated its terms on several occasions. For instance, Iran has test-fired a new missile capable of carrying multiple warheads. These warheads make the Little Boy dropped on Japan look like a roman candle in a child's hand on the Fourth of July. Then, a few months later, they fired two ballistic missiles with long-range capabilities. Again, they test-fired missiles known as "zero error" missiles, which are accurate to within twenty-five feet of their target. These missiles can travel over 2,000 kilometers (1,250 miles), which means they can easily reach Eastern Europe, Turkey, Saudi Arabia, Israel, and Yemen.[5]

While Iranian leaders dismiss the idea that any of these missile tests

are in violation of the agreement, they are indeed in direct contraven-
tion of the UN Resolution that governs the "deal." UN Security Council's Resolution 1929 indicates, "Iran shall not undertake any activity
related to ballistic missiles."[6] Then the Joint Comprehensive Plan of
Action agreement (JCPOA) states, "All these restrictions shall apply
until the date eight years after the JCPOA Adoption Day (18 October
2015) or until the date on which the IAEA submits a report confirming
the Broader Conclusion, whichever is earlier."[7] They barely waited eight
weeks!

What is their ultimate objective? The Iranian government is dedicated to the goal of dominating the world with what it considers to be
the true Islam. They'll stop at nothing to bend circumstances to this
aim.

The ayatollah enforces the law. He imposes rules about what a
woman can wear. He decrees what people can eat. He dictates the pa-
rameters of behavior and determines what is and what is not morally
acceptable. The punishment for breaking his law is extreme and, in
many cases, sees the offender publicly executed in the most graphic
manner.

I point this out because often people make the naive suggestion,
"Why not continue talking with them?"

Answer: because doing so is futile. They have already demonstrated
to the world that an agreement with them is really no agreement at all.

Others then interject, "Well, it worked in the Cold War."

The Cold War was a conflict with an entirely different ideological
group. While Communist Russia may have been ruthless and aggres-
sive, their government was tied to atheism, which meant the citizens
were told their government was god and the state was its church. Add
to that the Cold War concept of "mutual assured destruction,"[8] which

held that if you fire a nuclear bomb at them then they will fire one at you. This would ensure that both parties would not survive. Since the majority of the Russian people had no belief in the afterlife, their desire to remain alive on this planet was pretty strong.

Also, we had different leaders during the Cold War. The top priority of President Ronald Reagan was to take care of the American people, not to apologize for being American, such as we've seen from a later administration. It was a different time entirely.

Iran follows a religion that says that to die in the fight to establish the faith is the most desirable way to go. It holds to the idea of an Islamic messiah who will come to earth only in a state of extreme chaos and jihad (holy war). When Iranian President Ahmadinejad came to New York City on September 15, 2005, he asked the diplomats he met, "Do you know why we wish to have chaos at any price?" Then he answered his own question: "Because after the chaos, we shall see the greatness of Allah."[9] This is not a mind-set you can reason with.

Yet it is the mind-set that will carry into history's final conflicts, with Israel's enemies seeking her elimination. We don't know exactly when or to what extent nuclear weapons will be used. We do know that the whole world will not be destroyed, because Christ will return before the end. But one way or another, the "plague" of nuclear destruction *will* be unleashed in the violence of the end times.

COUNTDOWN

The human race has never made a weapon it did not intend to use. If the A-bomb dropped on Japan killed hundreds of thousands, then the warheads in the world today will no doubt kill millions. Christ told His disciples that they would hear of wars and rumors of war. Daniel said that knowledge would increase. Zechariah described a plague. Today's headlines say Iran is pursuing a nuclear weapon, while the world watches, thinking our concern and disapproval will be enough to make them stop.

All of these events fit together like finely tuned gears in a watch, turning the hour, minute, and second hands as it counts down to the day when the prophecy is fulfilled: "This shall be the plague."

13

LETTERS FOR SEVEN CHURCHES—AND US

Blessed is he who reads and those who hear the words of this prophecy,
and keep those things which are written in it; for the time is near.

—Revelation 1:3

Near the end of his life, the apostle John—one of Jesus's twelve original disciples—was exiled by the political authorities to the island of Patmos off the western coast of Asia Minor, or what today is known as Turkey. While he was on the island, he received the visions that he recorded as the book of Revelation. As we've seen, God has lifted the veil on the end times periodically throughout history, giving glimpses of what is to come through dreams to foreign kings, visions to Jewish prophets, and sermons by Jesus. But there was no more detailed or more extensive unveiling than what John received on Patmos, and therefore it is to the book of Revelation that we will turn in the final chapters of this book.

But I need to point out something that you may never have thought about before. Starting with chapter 4, the book of Revelation focuses primarily on events that will happen after the Rapture. Or to put it another way, believers who are living today will not go through these later experiences that will take place on earth—the Great Tribulation, the deception of the world by the Antichrist, the Battle of Armageddon,

Christ's return to defeat the forces of evil, and so on. Of course it's good to know about these things, but since *Your Guide to the Apocalypse* is an introductory book on the apocalypse, designed to teach believers in this final generation what they urgently need to know, we will not be focusing on these later events. Instead, we'll be focusing on the first three chapters of the book of Revelation, specifically the letters that the risen Jesus dictated for seven churches in the Roman province named Asia. Jesus said to John, "'I am the Alpha and the Omega, the First and the Last,' and, 'What you see, write in a book and send it to the seven churches which are in Asia: to Ephesus, to Smyrna, to Pergamos, to Thyatira, to Sardis, to Philadelphia, and to Laodicea'" (Revelation 1:11).

Over the next seven chapters, we'll be scrutinizing each of these letters in turn for what they teach us about the apocalypse and how we should be living in light of the imminence of Christ's return for us. Christ has expectations for how His followers will live as we wait for His return, and the seven letters show us what these expectations are.

LEVELS OF RELEVANCE IN THE SEVEN LETTERS

As simple as they may seem on the surface, the seven letters actually are rich in meaning and apply in more ways than one. To prepare you for the upcoming chapters, let me explain how we'll be looking at three levels of relevance in the messages that Jesus gave to the seven churches.

Situational Relevance
First, the messages pertained to the particular situations of those seven churches at that time.

Historical Relevance

Second, the seven churches represent a historical order. Just like the different sections of Nebuchadnezzar's statue, and just like the series of beasts that Daniel saw, the seven churches reflect a specific sequence of time periods. In this case, they represent a series of seven different ages in church history.

If you begin with the day of Pentecost, when the Holy Spirit founded the church, to the present day, there has been one church, but it has gone through various stages, each with its own defining characteristics. What John probably didn't realize, but what we can now see from our vantage point in history, is that the seven churches of Asia previewed the Christian eras.

Here's what makes this most meaningful for our purposes. In the seven ages, we see a relentless, unstoppable drive toward the end of history as God has ordained it. As we study each letter in turn, we'll sense the end times drawing ever nearer. Today we live in the last age of the church—the Laodicean Age. And not just the last age but the last moments of the last age! So again, just as with Nebuchadnezzar's statue and Daniel's beasts, the sequence of the seven letters gives us confirmation that we are indeed living at the end times and can expect the Lord to return for us at any moment to begin the finalizing of history.

Personal Relevance

Third, the seven letters also present themes that are relevant, not just to a particular church that no longer exists, and not just to an era in church history, but to all believers individually. So as we look at these letters, I will be pointing out theological and moral truths we can apply to ourselves.

As I hope you have already begun grasping, the apocalypse is not just a fascinating topic to read about. Its nearness and inevitability should cause us to reflect on how we're living today, seeking to obey the Lord in our own lives and in our churches so that we represent a vital witness to those around us who are separated from God by unbelief. The world needs Christ's light in a dark time.

The Seven Letters to the Churches of Asia		The Seven Ages of the Christian Church
The letter to the church of Ephesus (Revelation 2:1–7)	1	The apostolic church (AD 30–100)
The letter to the church of Smyrna (Revelation 2:8–11)	2	The church during Roman persecution (AD 100–312)
The letter to the church of Pergamos (Revelation 2:12–17)	3	The church in the age begun by Constantine (AD 312–606)
The letter to the church of Thyatira (Revelation 2:18–29)	4	The church during the prominence of the papacy (AD 606–1520)
The letter to the church of Sardis (Revelation 3:1–6)	5	The church of the Reformation (AD 1520–1750)
The letter to the church of Philadelphia (Revelation 3:7–13)	6	The church of the missionary movement (AD 1750–1900)
The letter to the church of Laodicea (Revelation 3:14–22)	7	The church of apostasy (AD 1900–present)

THE REALITY OF ACCOUNTABILITY

When it comes to obeying Christ, this is not some it's-nice-but-not-necessary message. There are two underlying themes in Revelation that should wake us up to the supreme and eternal importance of living as God commands in the light of the approaching apocalypse.

Jesus Is Watching What We Are Doing

Like a refrain that accompanies every verse of a song, the first underlying theme involves something that Jesus said in every one of the seven letters. And because He repeated it so consistently, we know that we had better pay attention to it. He said to the churches (and to us), "I know your works" (Revelation 2:2, 9, 13, 19; 3:1, 8, 15).

We live in an age when we feel justified in telling someone else, "Don't judge me!" or "You don't know my story" or "You don't understand my heart!" I believe that, when you are talking to another imperfect human being, all of those statements are true. But be mindful that there is Someone who knows all of those things and then some.

To every one of the seven churches, Christ said clearly, "I know. I know every time you went the extra mile for Me. I know all that you sacrificed and gave for the kingdom. I know every effort you made to comfort the afflicted, to love the unwanted, to help those in need." Similarly, even though we may think that nobody else is paying attention or cares about what is going on in our lives, Christ has a direct message for us: "I know."

Often we get frustrated when it seems that our successes are forgotten and our failures are magnified. The encouragement sent to the seven churches of Asia was, "I am watching what you do, and I know all about it." For those who are abiding by His Word and doing His will, these words are of great encouragement. God knows. He hears. He sees. That is why we are instructed in the Word, "Whatever you do, do all to the glory of God" (1 Corinthians 10:31).

And for those who are not doing what the Lord has commanded, Jesus has a word of warning: "I know your works. I know all about the sins you have been hiding. I know how you've forsaken the message of the gospel. I know how you have adapted to the popular opinions of others rather than telling them that My Word is unchanging."

"I know." Two words that, depending on individual behavior, will either bless and encourage you or send chills running down your spine.

Judgment Is Coming Soon

In one of the seven letters, Jesus said, "I am coming quickly!" (Revelation 3:11). Later, Jesus would repeat and expand this truth, saying, "I am coming quickly, and My reward is with Me" (22:12). So the second of the underlying themes is that His return is imminent and His reward will accompany His arrival.

One of the main reasons people like to dismiss the topic of prophecy is the awareness that they are going to have to give an account of how they lived on this earth. That disturbs them. But at least it shouldn't be a surprise. For thousands of years, the Bible has said clearly, "It is appointed for men to die once, but after this the judgment" (Hebrews 9:27). The question is not if you will be judged; the question is at which judgment bar you will stand—the judgment of the just or the judgment of the unjust.

The book of Revelation speaks of the "great white throne" of judgment where people will stand before Jesus Christ (Revelation 20:11). This will take place after the earth is no more and before the new heaven and the new earth have been created. The times of tribulation are over. The resurrection of the just (those who accepted Christ) and the unjust (those who rejected Him) has taken place, and now all of mankind is standing before the great white throne, and the one who sits upon it is the Son of God Himself.

In that context Revelation 20:12 says, "I saw the dead, small and great, standing before God, and books were opened. And another book was opened, which is the Book of Life." Isn't it interesting that God keeps two sets of books? One is filled with every thought, every word, and every deed for every person who ever lived and never accepted His Son as their Savior. The other is appropriately named the Book of Life, because those who find their name written in it are going to receive exactly that—life more abundant and eternal!

It is staggering to consider such an awesome sight. Pontius Pilate, who sentenced Jesus to death, will stand before Him. Judas, who kissed His cheek in betrayal, will be there too. The Caesars who persecuted the church, the Crusaders who burned synagogues, the inquisitors who ordered the Jews to convert or be exiled—all of them will be there.

In our modern world, we want to talk about Jesus as if He is fully willing to accept us on our terms. In truth, because He is the Creator and we are the created, we have no terms; there is only His will. His will is that we would believe in our heart and confess with our mouths that He is Christ the Lord and then follow His Word. Jesus said in John 5:27 that the Father "has given [the Son] authority to execute judgment also, because He is the Son of Man." That means that, because Christ came to earth and lived in the flesh and knows what it is like to struggle as a human struggles, He has the perfect knowledge to be able to judge all human flesh. You may think you have a good enough excuse for your friends and acquaintances here on earth as to why you are the way you are, but on judgment day you will not be explaining yourself to them.

Jesus continued His explanation: "Do not marvel at this; for the hour is coming in which all who are in the graves will hear His voice and come forth—those who have done good, to the resurrection of life, and those who have done evil, to the resurrection of condemnation" (John 5:28–29). There are only two options on that day—eternal life in the Paradise of God, or eternity in the lake of fire. That is why the scenes describing judgment day are of weeping and wailing and gnashing of teeth, because those who have no excuses will be fully aware that it's too late. It's really not hard to understand and it is simply a matter of choice. Believe on the Lord Jesus Christ and be saved, or refuse Him and face Him at the great white throne of judgment.

WHAT THE SPIRIT SAYS TO THE CHURCHES

Now let's turn to the letters to the seven churches. Remember, each letter was relevant to the specific church, relevant to the approach of the apocalypse, and relevant to us. We are about to learn what these churches did and see a picture of what many are doing today:

- losing their passion for seeing others come to faith (church of Ephesus)
- going through suffering (church of Smyrna)
- making compromises with pagan beliefs and practices (church of Pergamos)
- mixing the pure and the heathen (church of Thyatira)
- getting too comfortable and losing hunger for God (church of Sardis)
- learning to rely on God and remain faithful (church of Philadelphia)
- becoming lukewarm for Christ (church of Laodicea)

Each of the seven letters ends with the warning, "He who has an ear, let him hear what the Spirit says to the churches" (Revelation 2:7, 11, 17, 29; 3:6, 13, 22). This is not a routine closing, like "Sincerely yours." It's an urgent call to pay attention. And it reminds us of how desperately important these seven messages are to those of us who stand on the cusp of the apocalypse. We not only need to understand God's unveiling of events in the end times; we also need to understand and apply what He tells us about how He wants us to live in the light of His truth.

14

EPHESUS: LETTING GO OF FIRST LOVE

I have this against you, that you have left your first love.

—Revelation 2:4

I have spent most of my thirty-eight years on earth in church. I grew up as a church kid, attended all the church events, have witnessed the comical, seen the remarkable, and disregarded the nonsensical. I can assure you of this fact: God is so real to me that I could not deny Him. I've seen Him touch lives, mend the broken, and do the miraculous, and I have felt His presence as real as a warm embrace. Yet I have also known many who have seen what I have seen, sat where I have sat, felt what I have felt, and have simply walked away as if it never happened.

Some of them are dear friends who I keep in contact with today. Others were there for a moment but seemed to simply disappear. Either way, they fit all too well the description of those who once claimed to love the Lord and then behave as if they never made that claim. It's tragic, to say the least, but every time I see it I think about what the letter to the church of Ephesus says: "You have left your first love" (Revelation 2:4). When you know the signs, you can see the behavior in the world around you pointing directly to the fact that He's coming back.

As strange as it may sound, even when others deny Him, that's a clear indicator that the end is near.

PRAISE BEFORE CRITICISM

Let me point out something before we go any further.

In the letter to the church of Ephesus, we begin to see a pattern that Jesus maintains generally through all seven letters—He compliments before He corrects. Although He is not pleased with some things, He's not passive either. He finds a way to point out something good about a group of people who are doing some things wrong.

Jesus Christ was perfect and is certainly justified in telling every person in every church what they should correct. However, He first builds them up with love and encouragement before He points out anything else. In the case of Ephesus, He praised the church's hard work, persistence, and hatred of false teaching, but He nevertheless pointed out that the church had begun to lose its first love.

I find it encouraging that the Son of God sees the good in everyone, even those who desperately need to change. So let's pause for a moment and consider what we can learn from this.

Christ's pattern gives a great example for anyone who needs to confront a person regarding a matter that needs to change. Think about it: If the only perfect Being ever to walk the face of the earth set this as a pattern, don't you think it would be wise to implement the same practice in your relationships? Sooner or later you are going to have to confront someone. When you do, take the time to point out something you see in him or her that is good before you get to the matter at hand.

Now let's get to the letter to the Ephesians, the first in a series that marches toward the apocalypse. In what way does Jesus's praise or censure in this letter apply to us? Apply to our churches? In particular, if it was possible for churches to begin losing their passion for the Lord already at the beginning of church history, how much more possible is it for us? What does the condition of our heart say about our relationship with Christ and our readiness for His return?

LABORING DILIGENTLY FOR THE LORD

One of the qualities of the church at Ephesus that pleased the Lord was their effort on His behalf. He said, "I know your works, your labor, your patience, and that you cannot bear those who are evil" (Revelation 2:2).

The wording in this creates a separate understanding of the words *work* and *labor*. Work is something that requires effort and is done on occasion; labor is work that is done with intense exertion over a long period of time. Labor is the kind of work that makes one weary. There are people in every church who, at times, work, and then there are others who are laboring for the cause of Christ.

At Cornerstone Church I am constantly humbled by the faithful members who have given twenty, thirty, and even in some cases forty years to the constant work of the ministry. They don't volunteer for a month and then ask when they will receive their plaque of appreciation; they come Sunday after Sunday, rain or shine, and they serve. They serve, not for recognition, but out of a humble heart of gratitude for the Savior who cleansed them of their sin and unrighteousness. Some of them serve in the nursery, others in the choir, still others as ushers and greeters or in the parking lot. They do what they do with an attitude and spirit of excellence. It is an honor to be able to speak of them as members of our church, and I am privileged to be known as one of their pastors. Their acts of service may at times be overlooked by the masses, but this one verse is of great encouragement to all who fit the description because they are being told plainly that God in heaven sees what they do.

I said in the previous chapter that Jesus knows our works and is coming soon with His reward. Doesn't it make sense to consider how we are working and laboring for Him?

Every coach who is striving to win a game wants to make sure his or her best players are in the action just before the final whistle blows. Every relay team that wants to finish first puts the fastest runner in the anchor leg of the race so this athlete can cross the finish line victorious. Every World Series baseball team knows the value of a good "closer"—the pitcher who can assure a win in the final innings. Think of those examples in light of our topic. You and I are running the anchor leg of the race that Peter and John started. We, for some reason in God's providence, have been picked as the "closers" for the epic race that began in Genesis.

Our generation is playing during the two-minute warning . . . and then the time will run out. How are you going to finish? Full out or flat out? Working or wasting away? It's no accident you're here and it's no mistake that it's right now. The challenge that we must hold ourselves to is that, when the trumpet sounds, we leave the earth with sweat on our brow and our hands on the plow.

HATING WICKEDNESS

Jesus also complimented the church of Ephesus on the way they refused to tolerate evil. Said in modern terms, they had not forsaken the truth of the gospel for a popular social message that has substituted a lie for the truth. What could be more relevant and timely than this?

One of the greatest tragedies in the church today is that preachers are abandoning the truth. Pastors have chosen to be encouraging instead of effective. They would prefer to embrace a political correctness that apologizes for the convictions of our faith than to take a courageous stand for the gospel.

Christ, however, commended the church of Ephesus because they hated the deeds of the Nicolaitans. Who were these people? The Nicolaitans were a cult, a group claiming to be Christians but teaching and practicing things that were not consistent with biblical truth. We don't know much about what specifically they were promoting, but their name gives us a clue.

Nicolaitan comes from two Greek words. The first is *nike,* which means "victory"—hence the purpose behind the name of the popular sports line. (You didn't think they'd sell well if they named it after a bunch of losers, did you?) The second word is *laos,* which means "people." It's the same translation in which we get the modern word *laity. Nicolaitan* literally means "victory over people." So it seems we're talking about leaders who taught falsehood in the process of exalting themselves over the people in the church for the purpose of controlling them.

This is the exact opposite of what Christ commanded Peter to do. He asked His disciple, "Do you love Me?"

Peter responded, "You know that I love You."

Then Jesus said, "Feed My sheep" (John 21:17). Message: "Take care of My people."

Christ was a servant-leader, and He expected His followers to be the same. In Ephesus, however, they apparently had leaders who were more into being served than they were into serving. But the Ephesians weren't taking this sitting down. They hated the deeds of the Nicolaitans. This means they stood up against blatant evil and had no tolerance for it.

The Bible states, "You who love the LORD, hate evil!" (Psalm 97:10). In our modern world, it seems, the only thing one church is really good at hating is another church across the street. It should go without saying that it is a massive waste of energy for people of biblical values and faith to fight against each other when there is an entire world that is lost and dying and in desperate need of hope.

But notice that the Ephesian Christians did not hate the *people* in the Nicolaitan group. They hated the *deeds* of these misguided people. Plainly stated, hating a sinner is wrong and contrary to the example Christ set. The book of Romans reminds us that Christ loved us while we were yet sinners (see Romans 5:8). So we, as believers, must also love sinners even as we take a stand against the deeds of evil without apology.

We have made the church a passive place, but the church that Christ died to redeem was anything but passive. They were commissioned to take a stand in the evil day. Christ told His disciples that the gates of hell could not stand against the church that was willing to be vigilant in its stance against evil (see Matthew 16:18). When God looked at the church of Ephesus, He commended them for their willingness to resist the vile behavior that eroded the soul and corrupted society. If Jesus were to write a letter to your church today, would He be able to say the same?

KEEPING ON

Jesus continued praising the Ephesians by saying, "You have persevered and have patience, and have labored for My name's sake and have not become weary" (Revelation 2:3). Perseverance. Patience. Tireless labor. How rare these qualities are today! Yet the only way to accomplish a task is through the practice of patient endurance.

I have heard my father say on many occasions, "Talent may take you to the top, but discipline is the only thing that will keep you there." This world is full of talented people who do amazing things, and then as soon as they make their mark, they disappear, because they refuse to be patient and endure. The difference between history's boldest accomplishments and most staggering failures is simply the grit to be patient and endure.

The word "weary" in verse 3 is not the strongest translation of the original language. In the King James Version, the verse finishes with "and hast not fainted."[1] The reason "fainted" is more accurate is because "weary" is a broad term for becoming tired; "to faint," however, connotes degrees of action. Consider a car speeding down a road at eighty-five miles per hour. When it comes over a hill on the highway, the driver spots a police officer on a motorcycle holding a radar gun, and as soon as he sees him, the driver taps the brakes and slows down to fifty-five miles per hour. This is an example of "fainting" in speed. Similarly, a person who is running and then begins to walk is "fainting." The one who is walking and goes to sit is "fainting." And the one who sits and goes to lie down is, again, "fainting."

The message being communicated to the church in this letter is, "Don't slow down!" Keep up the pace—continue to work for God with the same zeal you had when you started.

But . . . a Cooling Heart

Then suddenly the tone of the message changes: "Nevertheless I have this against you, that you have left your first love" (Revelation 2:4).

The first love of the church is that of winning the lost to Christ. Consider the Great Commission: "Go into all the world and preach the gospel to every creature" (Mark 16:15). These words are not a suggestion; they are a direct order.

Everywhere the apostles went, they preached the gospel. They told everyone they encountered about Jesus Christ, the one who was crucified and rose again, and how faith in Him would give those who believed everlasting life. They taught new believers to have the same zeal for soul winning. But over time, this love for the lost began to wane.

The church in Ephesus was guilty of what many churches in the world today are guilty of—we have become so busy playing church that we've forgotten what it means to be a church. If we cease to win the lost to Christ and help those who are hurting, then we are no more than a social club gathering in the name of something holy. We cease to be a holy church gathering in the name of Jesus Christ, who died for our sins so we could be set free.

Jesus told the church of Ephesus, "Repent and do the first works, or else I will come to you quickly and remove your lampstand from its place—unless you repent" (Revelation 2:5). He told this church that they had a chance to make a choice, just like every person in every church today has the chance to do. They could choose to do what they knew was right, or they could choose to do what they wanted. If they chose to do what was right, they would be rewarded. If, however, they chose to do their own thing, they would be removed. Translation: they would no longer be effective for the cause of Christ and His kingdom here on earth.

How many churches do we see in the world today who have chosen their way instead of God's will? They no longer make a difference for the kingdom. Some may be doing good things, but are they doing God's thing? They may have a good reputation in their community, but what is God's opinion of their service to His Son? They may have had a rich history and done great things for God early on, but He is not evaluating them for who they were. He says, "Repent or else." He is warning them before it's too late.

Some hear the word "repent" and think that it's harsh and rude. The truth is, if an imperfect being were the one demanding repentance, then it might indeed be harsh, rude, and even hypocritical. But these words came directly from a perfect and loving God to people He truly cared for. Sometimes love's clearest voice is the voice of correction, the one that says, "Stop before it's too late!"

The message to the church of Ephesus was clear: *You started well, but you have drifted off course. Get back to being who you used to be— and do it now!*

I believe that, while the letter that was written to Ephesus hit them in the center of their heart thousands of years ago, it was also written to touch the hearts of many churches today. We have been warned. We must return to being who we are supposed to be instead of what the world wants us to be. With Christ's return imminent and judgment approaching fast, we must love everyone but take a stand against evil so that there is a clear distinction between what is right and what is wrong. Call it light and darkness if you like. Call it righteousness versus wickedness. But make sure that you do not slow down in your fervor for telling others about the love of Christ and what He has done for you.

15

SMYRNA: SUFFERING LIKE CHRIST

I know your works, tribulation, and poverty (but you are rich).

—Revelation 2:9

The second congregation in the lineup of Christ's seven messages is the church of Smyrna. Certain details in this brief letter might at first glance make it seem like John didn't understand what he was being told to write down, or that he simply wrote the wrong thing. How could a church that was known for their poverty be told they were rich? How could they be promised that they would suffer—at the hands of the devil himself, no less—and yet if they would remain faithful they would receive the "crown of life" (Revelation 2:10)? Smyrna clearly shows us the paradoxes in what happens when God's people go through hard times.

As with the church of Ephesus, the Lord wanted the believers of Smyrna to know that He knew what they were going through. He said, "I know your works, tribulation, and poverty" (verse 9). A more appropriate word than "tribulation" would be "suffering," and suffering is indeed the central focus of this letter.

As pastors know, certain topics will bring an audience with eager ears to hear them. If you preach on miracles, it's standing room only. If you inspire with a message of hope, everyone goes home feeling better about tomorrow. When you cover the topic of marriage and family, wives may have to drag husbands to the pew, but they will be there because, after all, most spouses want a better marriage. Out of all of the good advice I have received about preaching, no one has ever told me, "Pastor Matt, you should preach a sermon series titled 'Get Ready to Suffer.'" That, however, is exactly what Jesus Christ told John to write to this church.

Suffering is something that all of us experience. And it's something we should expect more frequently as we go through the birth pangs of the apocalypse.

It can be difficult to see beyond our immediate surroundings at times, but take a step back and look at how the suffering of Christians has been surging around the world. Radical regimes are committing hideous atrocities against men, women, and children for the "crime" of being a Christian. We have heard and seen what ISIS is doing to those who identify themselves as followers of Christ. For decades, certain governments around the globe have been hostile toward the church, often forcing them underground by forbidding them to assemble in public or to openly evangelize and welcome others into their fellowship. Without question, in many places around the world today, the church is suffering.

In America we may not want to consider it, but think about how popular it is to mock Christianity and those who follow Christ. In our hypersensitive culture, if you say anything contrary to someone's core values and beliefs, you are disdained for prejudice. Yet the same audience that accuses you of prejudice will applaud you for "relevance" and "boldness" if you turn your criticism toward Christians or the church.

The topic of persecution and suffering is a reality for believers around the world today and is something that the faithful should be mindful of the closer we get to the Rapture. It's not a matter of *if* we will suffer; it is a matter of *how* will we respond when suffering happens. Smyrna shows us the way to look at—and persist through—the hard things we experience.

TEN "DAYS" OF MARTYRDOM

In Smyrna, the believers in Christ were apparently suffering persecution from some in the local Jewish community—specifically, those who believed they were following the God of Abraham, Isaac, and Jacob but who actually showed they were more aligned with the devil by making life hard for the followers of the Messiah and Son of God, Jesus. Apparently they were using their influence with the local authorities to get some of the Christians thrown in jail.

But as we think about the persecution that the Christians of Smyrna were facing, we need to realize that Christ was talking about something bigger. In fact, at that time persecution of Christians was growing all around the Roman Empire and would get much worse before it got better. There is a hint of the long ordeal that lay ahead in this second letter of Revelation.

Christ said, "You will have tribulation ten days" (Revelation 2:10). By saying "days," He was not referring to ten twenty-four-hour periods. These ten "days" are ten historical periods under ten Roman emperors who hated Christians and the idea of Christianity. It began with the Roman emperor Nero in AD 54 and ended with Diocletian in AD 305. Within that period of time, there were ten Roman emperors who ruled Rome and persecuted and martyred Christians wherever they were found.

Consider the emperor who started it all. If anything went wrong in Rome—a natural disaster, earthquake, volcanic eruption, famine, pestilence, or plague—Nero would tell the Roman citizens that the Roman gods were angry because so many people were turning to Christ. Everything was the Christians' fault. (Does that political tactic sound familiar?)

Nero was merciless. He would have the bodies of Christians wrapped in oil-soaked rags and hung in the air, used as living torches so he could see his rose garden at night. Nero was so sadistic that he actually ordered a section of Rome to be set on fire. The fire ended up raging out of control for nearly three days. Three of Rome's fourteen districts were wiped out; only four were untouched by the tremendous conflagration. Hundreds of people died in the fire and many thousands were left homeless. Nero blamed the Christians for it all.

When the church was told that the devil himself was going to be the source of their tribulation, it wasn't an exaggeration. Nero was a living devil. And the Roman emperors who followed him were much the same. They put some of the most faithful people to the most horrendous deaths.[1]

Paul and Peter

The two best-known apostles each died a martyr's death. On June 29, AD 67, Paul the apostle was taken about three miles outside the city of Rome and then beheaded. Later, Peter was arrested and condemned to die by crucifixion. His request to his death squad was that he be crucified upside down, because he didn't feel worthy to die right side up as his Lord and Savior Jesus Christ had died.

Ignatius

Ignatius, the second pastor of the church in Antioch of Syria, was arrested, sent to Rome, and fed to the lions in the Colosseum. Why? Because he publicly confessed that Christ lived in his heart. This same profession of faith that is celebrated at every baptism service today cost this man his life in a gruesome and horrific way. History records how one hundred thousand screaming spectators cheered as Ignatius was eaten by starving lions, and when they were done, all that was left were two large bones.

Polycarp

Polycarp, the pastor of the church in Smyrna, at the age of eighty-six was arrested by Roman soldiers and commanded by the proconsul to "... reproach Christ." Seeing this as a denial of his faith, he refused. Enraged by his stubbornness, they stripped him naked in the public square, tied him to a large stake, and piled wood around it. They lit a fire, and the flames formed a large arch around his naked body.

When the Roman proconsul who ordered the execution saw that Polycarp's body wasn't being burned, he demanded he be run through with a sword. Accordingly, the elderly man's body was pierced, but the blood gushed from his wound and extinguished the flames. The onlookers were amazed. Polycarp died, but his death gave glory to Christ.[2]

The pagan followers may have been in power on earth, but God in heaven was the only Lord and there was none other.

Perpetua

Perpetua was a young Roman mother with an infant child who had converted to Christianity. She was ordered to sacrifice to the pagan gods and refused. She said, "I am a Christian and cannot deny Christ."

She was taken to the Colosseum, stripped naked, and suspended in a net. Hanging two feet off the ground, she was swung again and again into the brass-tipped horns of a wild bull.

As the bull buried its horns in her broken body and life was being taken from her in front of the crowd, her hair fell down from the traditional bun that she wore it in. She screamed for the execution to stop. Believing that she was going to recant her faith, the executioners contained the bull and let Perpetua out of the net. She then took her hair and put it back in its place, saying that letting hair hang down was a sign of mourning. She was not mourning; she was rejoicing that she had the privilege of dying for her Savior. She lay herself back in the net and was ravaged by the animal until her body was no longer recognizable as human.[3]

LIVING AND DYING FOR JESUS

In our world today, there are indeed graphic images of Christians who are suffering horrifically for their faith. They are being crucified, burned, beheaded, and tortured, but they will not deny Christ. More than 7,100 believers were killed for "faith-related reasons" in 2015 alone.[4]

Yet many of us who are blessed to live in a free and democratic republic are not being asked if we are willing to die for our faith, but rather if we are willing to live for it. In the Western world, where freedom of religion has been a staple of our society, we know little of the tribulations the early believers experienced. Nor do we experience the persecution Christians in some parts of the world face today. We see what's happening in the world, and while we are horrified at the thought, it is still far enough away that we are not confronted with it on a daily basis. But what do we do with the opportunity we have to share our faith with others? How have we taken advantage of the liberty that we have been afforded to profess Christ and not suffer for it?

In America, we feel as though we are suffering when someone says something mean about us. Do unkind words hurt? Sure, they do. But if they could kill you, I would not have lived to see my twenty-first birthday. Some have been taught that if you follow Christ and His teachings and live a life of faith, you will never suffer. Let me say this as directly as I can: that is not true! Tell that to Perpetua when you see her in heaven and see what she has to say.

Suffering is real, and so is the crown of life that comes to those who remain dedicated to Christ no matter what price they must pay.

CAUSES OF SUFFERING

We all suffer in a variety of ways. Persecution is just one of them. We all know what it's like to have accidents, illnesses, setbacks, disappointments, and griefs. As we prepare to remain faithful to Christ until He returns, how should we think about and react to our hardship? We need to understand what is going on when we suffer.

There are several reasons why people suffer.

Poor Choices

Don't ever forget it—choices have consequences. God's grace can work out the trouble you've caused with bad decisions so that your life is not ruined, but the effects of the choices you made will still remain.

David was called a man after God's own heart (see Acts 13:22), but David chose to have an affair with Bathsheba. He chose to try to cover his sin instead of confessing it. He chose to murder Bathsheba's husband when his first plan didn't work. David, in his pride, probably thought, *I did it. I got away with murder. No one knows what I've done. I look like a gracious king for marrying the widow of Uriah, and I will never have to tell.* But remember what God said to the churches of Asia: "I know your works."

God sent the prophet Nathan to see David. This prophet pointed his finger in the face of the king, and speaking on behalf of the Judge of all mankind, told David, "You are the man!" (2 Samuel 12:7). David was caught from day one by God Almighty.

His consequence? The sword never left his house. One of his sons, driven by lust, raped his sister, David's daughter. That son was killed by another of David's sons, Absalom. The child that David conceived with Bathsheba died shortly after he was born. Absalom was killed trying to lead a revolt against his father, David. Finally, David was forbidden from doing what he had desired to do for God—build His temple. Why? Because choices have consequences and David suffered for the foolish choices he made.

God in His grace and mercy forgave David when he repented. He did not take David's life, although He could have. He did not take David's throne, although He could have. God allowed David's second-born son with Bathsheba, Solomon, to build the temple and to be known as the richest man in the world. Did David deserve that? Absolutely not! But our God is a gracious God. And yet David did suffer because of his own choices, which he never forgot and deeply regretted.

Ignorance

Another reason people suffer is their ignorance. They simply don't know any better, and since they are uninformed, they continue to suffer instead of trying to find a better way.

Earlier I told you how my grandfather's parents buried four infant sons during the flu pandemic of 1918–20. Many considered it to be the incurable plague. In reality, the cure was not being sought because scientists accepted the false notion that influenza was caused by bacteria. Even though the researcher who believed he had discovered the flu bacillus had failed to provide definitive proof, his conclusions were seldom questioned and widely accepted.[5] Then, in the midst of the flu pandemic, doctors performing autopsies on those who had died from the flu couldn't find any trace of bacteria in the victims' bodies or blood. It wasn't until 1938 that the bacteria myth was debunked and the first flu vaccines were created by Jonas Salk and Thomas Francis.[6] For years people suffered and died due to ignorance.

The Sovereign Purposes of God

The third reason people suffer is because of the sovereign purposes of God that are unknown to man. This is why we are told, "Trust in the LORD with all your heart, and lean not on your own understanding" (Proverbs 3:5). That word "lean" paints the picture of someone using a crutch. We cripple ourselves when we try to understand God on our own terms. He is not like us. "For as the heavens are higher than the earth," the Lord says, "so are My ways higher than your ways, and My thoughts than your thoughts" (Isaiah 55:9).

Look at what happened to the church during times of suffering. It grew. The more they were persecuted, the faster people came to the faith. The more Rome tried to snuff them out, the more passion and fire grew for Christianity. That is why God told the believers of Smyrna, "You are rich."

But for the church in Smyrna, it wasn't earthly wealth. Rome confiscated all their possessions. Then how were they rich? Where was their reward? It was an eternal savings account, which they were going to enjoy much longer than any material wealth they could have ever enjoyed while they lived on this earth.

The day will come when all you will have to enjoy in eternity is what you gave to God while you were here on earth. "Lay up for yourselves treasures in heaven," Jesus urges us, "where neither moth nor rust destroys and where thieves do not break in and steal" (Matthew 6:20). This is a reminder that, no matter what you have on earth, the moment you possess it, you start to lose it. If it's a nice garment, a moth will eat it eventually. If it's priceless gold or gems, you'd better buy a vault, because a thief will attempt to steal it from you. If it is a great house or nice car, it only ages, rusts, and decays the longer you hold on to it. The only way you can truly have it forever is if you allow God to use it before it's too late.

This church was rich because they gave all they could when they had the chance, and God told them, "Do not fear" (Revelation 2:10). They had no reason to fear, because while they suffered, God was with them. He is an ever-present help in a time of trouble. This and other Bible verses remind us that in our darkest hours God is by our side. Not only was He with them while they suffered here on earth, but when they breathed their last breath, His was the first face that greeted them. The first thing He did was wipe away every tear from their eyes.

FROM HERE TO ETERNITY

All of my life I have heard family members and elders in the church have coffee-cup discussions about the end times. Often I would shudder as a child when I'd hear someone I knew well and trusted say something like, "You know, in the last days things will grow worse and worse." Some would begin to speculate how many pastors will be imprisoned and how many will fall away. Because I came from a long line of pastors and expected to become one myself, I would wonder what my jail cell would look like and how long my sentence would be. Ridiculous, I know. But remember, I was a child listening to what others were describing as an unavoidable reality.

Today I have a different attitude about this.

Jesus said to His disciples, "Do not worry about tomorrow, for tomorrow will worry about its own things. Sufficient for the day is its own trouble" (Matthew 6:34). When it comes to the end times and persecution, I hold fast to the encouragement that came to those in Smyrna: "Do not fear" (Revelation 2:10).

Don't worry about whether persecution will come to you. Don't be afraid if you have to go through fiery trials. Remember that this world is not your home or your reward. Your purpose here is to live in such a way that you will enjoy what you receive when you enter eternity.

That doesn't mean there is nothing worth celebrating here and now. Neither does it mean you should be concerned with certain doom. It means to take every day and consider it a gift from God and use it in such a way that what you do with your time is your gift back to Him.

The church that suffered in Smyrna honored the Lord because they refused to quit shining. May we learn from their example and be willing to shine, in the good or the harsh times, until we hear, "Well done, good and faithful servant. . . . Enter into the joy of your lord" (Matthew 25:21, 23).

PERGAMOS: TEMPTED BY COMPROMISE

I have a few things against you, because you have there those
who hold the doctrine of Balaam. . . . You also have those
who hold the doctrine of the Nicolaitans.

—Revelation 2:14–15

We are always willing to consider the lives of others when it comes to areas of improvement, but we typically create excuses about the places where our lives lack. So as we see the church nearing the final moments of history, we should consider the Bible verse that says, "Examine yourselves as to whether you are in the faith" (2 Corinthians 13:5). The church of Pergamos lost sight of this truth and it cost them dearly. They fell into the trap of comparing themselves against each other rather than the truth of God's Word.

Can you identify anywhere this is taking place among believers today? They consider the conduct of others to be the standard that measures whether or not they are faithful. "Well, I'm not as bad as Charlie. He tells slanderous lies; all I do is gossip a little." This kind of logic is not only terribly flawed, but it also points to an attitude that will be present among Christians until the trumpet sounds. "I am not as bad as the rest of them, so I must be okay!"

We live in an age when many people who claim to follow Christ are willing and even eager to compromise godliness with worldliness. They encourage others to do the same and look down on them if they don't. This is the opposite of the faithfulness Christ will look for when He comes back. Such compromise has been present in every generation of the Christian church, but its prevalence in our day is definitely consistent with the fact that we are now primed for the end to come.

Will we go along to get along, or will we hold out? The pull to make life easier and more enjoyable for ourselves by going along with worldly values and interests is powerful. Christ's letter to the church in Pergamos tells us what to do if we have been tempted to compromise, so that we can remain ready for Jesus to return any day.

History says He's soon to return. The modern State of Israel points to the fact that it could be any hour. The signs of the time in our culture say nothing is missing. The question is, Is this really the time that we should be playing spiritual games with a loving God who has called us to be faithful?

As a teacher of the Bible, I have a responsibility to point out the truth that is found in the Word. As a pastor, I am obligated by the One who called me to make sure you have the opportunity to prepare for the moment when you meet Him. So let me tell you that this letter to Pergamos has as much to do with self-examination and preparation as any other topic. It reflects the same relative approach to the faith that is being applied in our world and culture today.

No Excuses

Pergamos was the largest fortified city in the province of Asia in what is today western Turkey. All of the Roman military supplies for the region were shipped there. All of the Roman governors of the province lived there, and Roman business was carried out in the government buildings of Pergamos.

In fact, everything that Rome had to offer could be had in Pergamos. It was a city filled with idol worship and prostitution. It was rampant with homosexuality. It was corrupt from top to bottom and inside and out.

Yet, in spite of all the corruption and debauchery, God did not lower His standards for the congregation of Jesus followers in this city. He didn't say, "I know where you live, and because it is a sinful place, you have a good excuse to be a sinful church." No. He said, "I know where you live and you have not denied My faith."

This is an important example for us to note. God not only knows our works; He also knows our surroundings. He is aware of the social pressures and temptations that the world attempts to overwhelm people of faith with.

Sometimes we want to create the excuse that the Bible is outdated when it comes to modern life, as if the moral standards of Scripture are too extreme or irrelevant to be carried out in the world we live in. Not true at all! In a heavily Roman-influenced city like Pergamos, immorality of a bold kind was common. For example, a man might take his wife and children to a theater for a show, and while they sat and watched the program, he would excuse himself to hire a prostitute of any age and either gender in the same theater where his wife and children currently sat. How ludicrous and crude! But you know, "When in Rome . . ."

The church in Pergamos was in a tough neighborhood, and God knew it. So He was proud of them for keeping the faith.

These days, we live in a tough neighborhood and a tough time for godliness too. Are we making God proud?

When we see the Lord, we will not be able to say to Him, "Well, they invented this thing called the Internet, and pornography was free and accessible all the time." Nor, "I was young and it was spring break and everyone was doing it!" Not even, "Man, it was the sixties. Who wasn't getting high?"

To the church of Pergamos—and to us—He says, "You can live next door to the devil himself, and I still expect you to live for Me."

STANDING ON THE WORD

A faithful church is a church that does not make excuses for bad behavior. They overcome evil with good. How did the faithful Christians of Pergamos do that? The same way we must do it in our morally corrupt modern world—take a stand! The world that the Pergameans were living in didn't know right from wrong, but the Christians did. They were surrounded by a moral fog, but they chose to use the Word of God as a lamp to their feet and a light to their path.

Notice the words written to the angel of the church of Pergamos in Revelation 2:12: "These things says He who has the sharp two-edged sword." Christ was telling every church that has ever gathered on any day for any reason that there is a weapon that can overcome the greatest of enemies, and that weapon is the Word of God. In Ephesians 6:17, Paul refers to the Word as being a sword. Later in Revelation, John sees the end of the Battle of Armageddon, and he describes heaven opening and Christ riding on a white horse with a sharp two-edged sword in His mouth, which is the Word of God (see Revelation 19:15). The church of Pergamos knew how to use what most churches in the world today ignore—the Word of God.

The Word is controversial. There is only one thing you can do with a sword, and that is cut! The Word cuts the hearts of men, reminds them of sin, and tells them why they need a Savior. We don't like the idea of our sin being our fault. We would rather explain away sin than forsake it. Swords cut out enemies as the declarations of truth and crush every lie that has ever been spoken.

Let me show you what this looks like.

Abortion is a lie. It is a lie that says that what is in the womb is not human; it's not alive; it has no rights. The Bible crushes that lie. God told Jeremiah,

Before I formed you in the womb I knew you;
Before you were born I sanctified you;
I ordained you a prophet to the nations. (Jeremiah 1:5)

How can you be known and ordained if you are not even a living being until after the fortieth week of gestation?

The Bible states that life is in the blood (see Leviticus 17:11). Science confirms that as early as eight days after conception the child in the womb has a heartbeat and blood that circulates. Therefore, the Word and science crush the lie that there is no life till birth. The two-edged sword of the Word of God clearly states, therefore, that abortion is murder, and according to His Word, those who commit murder will face the consequence. This may not be popular or politically correct, but God is not concerned with either when it comes to the difference between truth and a lie, right and wrong.

This is just one example of a controversial social issue in our world today, but the Bible leaves no stone unturned when it comes to cutting through the lies and getting to the heart of the matter. It's not a question of, do we have enough information from the book? It's a matter of, what do we do with the information we have?

THE SPIRIT OF BALAAM

God was proud of the Pergamean believers because they were willing to take a stand in a tough town. But the news wasn't all good. God says, "But I have a few things against you, because you have there those who hold the doctrine of Balaam" (Revelation 2:14). Balaam—now, that's a name that hasn't been heard since the days of Moses!

Who was Balaam and what did he do? The Old Testament story of Balaam and his donkey has been told and retold to the point that it is frequently the punch line for a preacher's pulpit joke. "You've heard that God could make a donkey talk. . . ." Well, Balaam did more than that. Balaam was indeed a prophet, and he really did have spiritual power. He was known in his time and region as a man who could speak such powerful words over people's lives that what he said came to pass.

We find the story in Numbers 22. At the time this chapter describes, Israel was marching toward the Promised Land and God was blessing them with a series of victories along the way. The next kingdom they were going to conquer was Moab, and Balak was the king over that land. Balak went to Balaam and said, "I will make you a very rich man if you will go and curse these people" (see verse 17). Balaam agreed despite God's warning not to. But finally God sent an angel who (with the help of the famous donkey) convinced Balaam that he could not curse what God had blessed.

Here's the key point for our purposes. In the end, Balaam did give

Balak some wicked advice. Balaam knew that if King Balak could convince the men of Israel to marry the women of Moab, these unions would create religious problems for the sons of Abraham. The covenant with God clearly stated, "You shall have no other gods before Me" (Exodus 20:3). If these Moabite women could get their newlywed husbands to start sacrificing to other gods, then God Himself could not bless Israel, and Balak would get what he wanted—a curse on God's people that they would bring on themselves through disobedience.

You might think this was pretty clever. Balaam and Balak get to have their cake and eat it too. Don't forget, however, that God always says, "I know your works." God hated what Balaam did then, and He hates it when others do similar things.

God has no tolerance when His people create opportunity for others to live in open rebellion against His law. It happened in Moab in the Old Testament age; it was happening with certain church leaders in Pergamos; and there is no doubt it is happening in churches all over the world today. We have sanctuaries full of people who are listening to preachers tell them that even if what they are doing is directly opposed to God's Word, it is permissible. They are saying that somehow God has changed His mind about the Ten Commandments and you suddenly have His approval not only to break the commandments but also not to have to repent about it. It's okay to live in adultery, even when God's Word says the only condoned sexual relationship is inside the covenant of marriage. We have preachers accepting homosexuality even though God said it's an abomination. We have messages that never address sin because we don't want anyone to be offended.

Don't be mistaken. The one who is offended the most by messages like these is God Himself. If God was going to kill Balaam for his behavior in the days of Moses, and He held that same behavior against the church of Pergamos, then I can assure you that God is taking down the names of every pastor who hides behind political correctness today and will hold it against them too.

TIMES OF COMPROMISE

The message to the church of Pergamos continues, "You also have those who hold the doctrine of the Nicolaitans, which thing I hate" (Revelation 2:15). This was the same group that the church in Ephesus despised. As you recall, these were leaders in a cult who were more interested in being served than they were in serving others. Theirs was a viewpoint that God detested.

So whether it was justification of idol worship and immorality (Balaam), or whether it was abuse of power (the Nicolaitans), the Christians of Pergamos were being tempted to compromise their godly faith and living.

Now let's consider the historical context. The church of Pergamos represents the era when the church married the world. It's called the Pergamean Church Age. It began when Emperor Constantine of Rome signed the Edict of Toleration.

Prior to this period, Christianity had suffered greatly during the rule of ten Roman emperors, from Nero to Diocletian. But Constantine was one of the Roman emperors caught in a civil war between the Eastern portion of the empire and the West. The night before a decisive battle, this pagan emperor claimed to have had a dream, and in this dream he saw a shield. On this shield he saw an emblem that he described as blue and white divided by a red cross. He believed that it was the cross of Christ and that if he were to fight under that emblem, he would be victorious. He ordered his army to paint the emblem on their shields and display it on their battle flags. History records how Constantine won the battle, reunited Rome, and claimed from then on that Christianity would become the official state religion of the empire.

The only problem was that Constantine never fully became a Christian. He practiced pagan rituals in the name of Christ. He filled Roman temples with statues of Christ and the disciples and began praying to the statues just as he had previously prayed to the Roman statues of gods and goddesses. And many others in his day were incomplete converts as well. They had ceremony but not sanctification. They had rituals but no righteousness.[1] Like Balak and Moab, they had married into what God had redeemed by blood and were corrupting what He had washed white as snow.

God hated it then and He hates it now. The Bible says, "Whoever . . . wants to be a friend of the world makes himself an enemy of God" (James 4:4).

As the apocalypse approaches, we are going to be tempted to make compromises with the world. Those of us who are looking for the return of Christ and want to be ready when He appears must separate from those who want to merge the church and the world. Not that we remove our witness and friendship from sinners, but we must determine to keep ourselves pure and faithful to the Lord and His Word.

The Way of Escape

Maybe to some degree you have already given in to the compromising spirit of twenty-first-century Christianity. If so, it's serious. But it's certainly not unforgivable. God's wonderful grace is active in these latter days and will be available right up to the end for those who are ready to turn from evil and turn toward God.

The final warning to Pergamos echoes in our churches today: "Repent, or else I will come to you quickly and will fight against them with the sword of My mouth" (Revelation 2:16). There's a way of escape amid the peril. We can repent and begin again in faithfulness as we wait for the Lord's soon return.

THYATIRA: TOLERATING FALSE TEACHING

I have a few things against you, because you allow that woman Jezebel,
who calls herself a prophetess, to teach and seduce My servants to commit
sexual immorality and eat things sacrificed to idols.

—Revelation 2:20

Do you ever wonder why people in our day aren't seeking to get things right with God before they die? One answer widely given is they just don't know any better. But ignorance of the law is no defense.

I recall the first time that I—as a new driver—got pulled over for a speeding ticket. As I waited for the officer to step up to my car window, I was already terrified of the consequence I would receive from the judge. How long would the sentence last, and would I ever be permitted on the roadways again? I knew for certain that, based on the severity of my violation, I was not only guilty but doomed.

Of course the judge that I am referring to was my father. As for the one down at the courthouse, he was a minor concern compared to the one who had already made it clear to me that I was to be responsible behind the wheel.

The officer appeared at the window. "How are you doing today?" he asked.

"Hello, sir. I'm fine, I guess. Was I doing something wrong?" I thought naive innocence might be the best approach. I even put a touch of tremble in my tone and allowed my voice to crack in a pubescent "Golly shucks" kind of way.

"I pulled you over today because you were speeding. Do you have any idea what speed I clocked you at?"

"No sir, I don't. Was I going a little too fast?"

"Oh, yeah, you were. Seventy-nine in a fifty is not a little over; it's big time!"

The words slammed against my soul like the ocean against sea cliffs. What did "big time" mean? Is this where they call for backup? Who do I place my one and only phone call to? So many decisions to make and so little time to process; it was overwhelming.

I did what any desperate sixteen-year-old would do who was watching his entire life slip into the abyss of restriction. "Sir, I promise I had no clue! I didn't know what I was doing. Can you please give me a warning?"

He cracked a sly smirk, and for a moment I thought, *This is working!* Then I heard the horrific sound of the tearing of carbon paper. "I am going to give you a ticket *and* a warning!"

"Wait, what?! How can you do that?"

He continued, "This is your ticket for speeding. Please sign the bottom and report to the courthouse on or before the listed date. Here is your warning: ignorance of the law is not a defense. Even if you didn't know you were doing wrong, it's still wrong. Drive carefully and more slowly, please."

I never forgot that warning. *Ignorance is no defense.*

In these last days, how many people do we find claiming ignorance? They apparently believe that "I didn't know!" will be an adequate account on judgment day.

As we consider the next letter, we should be mindful that we are responsible for our actions, not based on what we believe to be right and wrong, but based on what God's Word declares. We have no excuse, and claiming nobody told us will not be an adequate defense. If you don't believe me, take a look at what John was told to write to Thyatira.

The letter to Thyatira reminds us that false teaching is a problem that has plagued humanity since way back in its history. False teaching will be a problem at the end of time as well, when a figure known as the "false prophet" (Revelation 16:13) will join the beast (Antichrist) and Satan in an unholy trinity. But most urgently for us, we deal with false teachers and false teaching right now. To the extent that we allow untruth to influence us, we are pulled away from faithfulness to the Lord who is soon to return for us. Remember what Jesus warned His disciples about: "Take heed that no one deceives you" (Matthew 24:4).

Let's look at what Christ had to say to a church that was tolerating a false teacher. As usual, He started with the positive side of the picture.

What Was Going Right in Thyatira

Christ had a litany of praises for the believers of Thyatira. "I know your works, love, service, faith, and your patience," He said (Revelation 2:19). Each one of these virtues is worth emulating.

Works

There is a strong emphasis in the seven letters on works, labor, and deeds. The believers of Thyatira were producing the fruit of their faith. They were serving and obeying the Lord.

Love

Love is the currency of every exchange in the kingdom of God. If you do anything for God and you do not do it in love, then your effort is in vain. In the famous "love chapter," the apostle Paul wrote to the Corinthian church that if he had all knowledge, but didn't have love, he would be nothing. If he had great spiritual gifts, but didn't have love, his gifts would be worthless. And even if he gave his body to be burned, and didn't have love, it wouldn't matter (see 1 Corinthians 13).

Service

It's natural for this church to be commended for love and service in that order, because service is the by-product of love. The Bible is direct in pointing out that love is not what you say, but it is what you do. Jesus said to His disciples, "By this all will know that you are My disciples, if you have love for one another" (John 13:35). Love is action. It is so visible that it doesn't need to be explained and cannot be denied.

Faith

The church of Thyatira was also a church that possessed faith. Remember, without faith it is not possible to please God (see Hebrews 11:6).

Patience

They were considered persistent, enduring, and patient. They did not become discouraged if they didn't see instantaneous results in the work they were doing for the Lord. They continued to press on, believing that in time they would see a better outcome.

LESSONS FORGOTTEN

In Revelation 2:19 we learn so many lessons regarding this body of believers, many of which have been forgotten by our churches today. We know how we want to be treated, but we don't love one another enough to consider others before ourselves. We are, for the most part, self-centered, and we struggle with serving others. We can't do much for anyone else when we are more concerned about our own needs. Then, as far as faith is concerned, it seems many churches today will apply it to most everything other than God's Word. People have faith in hope, grace, the power of the mind, and personal wealth and prosperity, but the Bible says, "Faith comes by hearing, and hearing by the word of God" (Romans 10:17). Unless the Word is the source of your faith, you practice your faith in vain.

Our modern world has forgotten many of the things the church in Thyatira knew, especially persistence. If we don't get instant results, we give up and lay the blame on a lack of performance instead of an unwillingness to endure. If we pray in church and the prayer doesn't get answered before we get to the car, we want to claim that prayer doesn't work. If we volunteer and our hours of service are not rewarded with praise, we choose to be offended rather than serve anymore. If we don't get what we want when we want it and in the way we want it, we tell others, "I tried church, but it didn't make much of a change." If I may be blunt, you didn't give it enough time to make a change! You can't have years filled with problems and expect them to be reversed because you decided to drop by for a visit one

Sunday. You have to be patient. Give it some time. Be willing to work it out.

Yes, there is much that we could learn from Thyatira, but the Son of God has something else He would like to say.

THE NEW JEZEBEL

Christ dictated to John for the believers of Thyatira, "Nevertheless I have a few things against you, because you allow that woman Jezebel, who calls herself a prophetess, to teach and seduce My servants to commit sexual immorality and eat things sacrificed to idols" (Revelation 2:20).

This church knew there was false teaching taking place, and they allowed it. They were aware of the wrong within their walls, and they ignored it. For all they did right, it was what they were failing to address that caused the Son of God to look at them with eyes of fire and send a warning that could not be taken lightly. Bottom line, they may not have been responsible for the wrongdoing, but because they were not willing to stand against it, they were the ones who would suffer.

Presumably, Jezebel was not the real name of the false teacher in Thyatira. We don't know her real name. The issues involved in her doctrine seem to have been the same ones in Pergamos—making concessions for sexual immorality and being involved in idol worship. The name Christ gave her is suggestive of the character of this woman and the peril she represented for God's people.

In the history of Israel, Jezebel was the wife of King Ahab.[1] She brought Baal worship into the nation and demanded that worship of this idol replace the worship of Jehovah God at Israel's altars. And this Baal worship was no wholesome alternative to faith in the one true

God. Baal was considered the creator of all things. If you saw grass and trees growing in the field, it was the power of Baal that did that. When it rained, it was Baal who made it rain. When it was time for the harvest, thank Baal for the harvest. If your cow had a new calf, or your sheep had little lambs, or your wife had a new baby, that was all made possible by Baal.

Baal worship included the sacrificing of all that Baal had given you—plants, livestock, even children. Because Baal made everything fertile, you could go to the temple of Baal and have sex with your spouse if you wanted to have a child. There were festivals for Baal that were nothing less than massive orgies, and should someone become pregnant with a child at this hedonistic affair, she could take the child back to the temple after it was born and sacrifice it on an altar to show her appreciation to the one who had made it possible—Baal. The reason I point this out is because often people don't understand why these little statues, with people saying silly prayers to them, made God so upset. Baal worship was destroying what God had created and blessed!

You may say, "Well, that was a long time ago."

It was a perennial problem. A false teacher in Thyatira was introducing similar beliefs and practices there in the first century. And paganism is still common today.

Look around you. People practice the same behaviors that Jezebel endorsed in worshipping Baal. They worship trees and nature and have an entire culture devoted to creation, exalting it above human life. They engage in sex outside of marriage for the same carnal satisfaction that Baal worshippers did, and if they get pregnant, they run to a doctor's office, lie on a table, and sacrifice the life of the child in the womb to the god of self. We've changed the name, but the behavior is the same, and the Son of God still despises it.

The Ancient Origins of Jezebel's False Doctrine

When did the doctrine of Jezebel begin? It began early in human history, just a few generations after Noah.

In Genesis 10:8–11, we read about the great hunter and builder Nimrod. Historians tell us that Nimrod's wife was a woman named Semmerimus.[2] She claimed her son Tammuz was the one promised in Genesis 3:15 as the seed of the woman, the coming Messiah. Because of this belief, she made herself the high priestess of the Babylonian religion, and she and her son were the objects of worship. It was the first mother-child cult in the history of the world, and in its essence it never went away.

The way these types of cults work is that you must gain access to the messiah figure through the bidding of his mother. If you want him to do something for you, you should pray to her. After all, he will do whatever she tells him.

Semmerimus taught the people of Babel that she was the way to approach God. But the Bible teaches, "No one comes to the Father except through Me." Semmerimus said she was the one who gave life. Jesus said, "I am the way, the truth, and the life" (John 14:6). Semmerimus gave herself the title "Queen of Heaven." The Word clearly declares, "I am the LORD your God and there is no other" (Joel 2:27).

When you take the time to learn and understand the teachings of Babylonian theology, you then will see the fingerprints of its divisive and diabolical imprint all over our society and in today's religions. Let me give you just one example. In Jeremiah we read,

Do not learn the way of the Gentiles;
Do not be dismayed . . . at them.

For the customs of the peoples are futile;

For one cuts a tree from the forest. . . .

They decorate it with silver and gold. (10:2–4)

This was a Babylonian practice for a midwinter festival celebrating the birth of Tammuz. We might compare it to a Christmas tree that is decorated every December to celebrate the traditional date of the birth of Christ.

Now, before you boycott Christmas, let me say plainly that the Babylonians worshipped the tree itself because it was the symbol of their messiah. You don't have to do that with your Christmas tree. Some of my fondest memories are of sharing time with my family every Christmas, including enjoying a beautifully decorated tree in the center of our home with many wonderful gifts under it. We did not worship the tree, never have and never will, but we do give all glory to God for the fact that He sent His Son, who died on a tree, and that His death paid the price for our sins.

The point of this example is to show that the impact of this cult described in the book of Genesis is still real.

In Thyatira the pure works based on faith, patience, love, and service were being mixed with heathen behaviors that had a long and sullied pedigree. It was creating the same mother-child cult that began with Semmerimus and continued with Jezebel.

THE PATIENCE AND THE JUSTICE OF GOD

The letter continues, still referring to the Jezebel figure in Thyatira. "I gave her time to repent . . . and she did not repent" (Revelation 2:21).

Isn't it remarkable that, as much as God hates the behavior, He is willing to be patient, giving us time to see the error of our ways in order that we might change? So often people misinterpret what God is doing and why. If He does not instantly strike down a sinner, then humanity foolishly convinces itself that "God doesn't mind what we are doing." We don't take the time to consider that His long-suffering with our misconduct is not an endorsement of it but rather an opportunity for us to change before it is too late. When He sees us willfully sin, His eye becomes like flames of fire. It is not okay!

In verse 23, we read that Christ said, "I will kill her children with death." Jezebel's "children" were her followers. Those who *claim* Christ but do not *possess* Christ will not have a good ending.

The fear people have when they read strong passages like this is, *How will God know who is right and who is wrong? What if He judges the innocent with the guilty?*

He never has and He never will. Consider the conversation that God had with Abraham about Sodom and Gomorrah (see Genesis 18:16–33). Abraham wanted to know the same thing: would God kill the innocent with the guilty? In the discussion Abraham asked God to spare the city if there were fifty, twenty-five, or even ten people who were not guilty. God promised Abraham He would, and He sent angels to extract the only family that was not guilty—the family of Lot, Abraham's nephew. God is a righteous judge.

See how the letter draws to a close. "Now to you I say, and to the rest in Thyatira, as many as do not have this doctrine, who have not known the depths of Satan, as they say, I will put on you no other burden" (Revelation 2:24).

God knows our works. He knows what we do and why we do it. Seeing our motive, He is fully aware of who deserves judgment and who deserves reward. To see evil and not call it evil is evil! If you are not standing up against what is wrong, you are indeed allowing it to continue and therefore you are as guilty as those who are committing the evil.

Without question, the behavior of this church is applicable to what we see happening today. Many people want to live according to their standard rather than God's. Some are even brash enough to attempt to recruit others, and they use the logic that, because they haven't faced any real consequences, then it must be permissible in some way. The greatest misconception with this type of individual, or group of believers, is that Jesus described His return like that of a thief in the night. When many are not expecting it, He will come and the days of grace will be over. Like the door in Noah's ark, the opportunity for salvation from the flood will be closed and those on the outside will be left to face the rising tide of judgment.

The church in Thyatira had a lot of wonderful qualities but risked losing it all if they were not willing to confront the wrong and make it right. In many ways we must diligently do the same. God is consistent. If He required an answer of this church for their conduct, He will require the same of us. And remember that when we stand before the Judge, ignorance will be no defense before the law.

SARDIS: MORE DEAD THAN ALIVE

You have a name that you are alive, but you are dead.

—Revelation 3:1

E arlier I mentioned that Christ typically complimented before He corrected the churches of Asia. Here, however, I must point out an exception to the pattern. Eventually in the letter Christ will acknowledge that there were a few faithful people in Sardis, but starting out the letter, He gives no praise of any kind for this congregation. "I know your works," Christ says. "You are dead" (Revelation 3:1).

Remember, these seven letters tell the story of church history, depicting the behavior of the church from Pentecost until the return of Christ. Ephesus represents the early church that started in Jerusalem at Pentecost and grew quickly, going from house to house and having favor with God and man. Smyrna was the persecuted church that was tortured by Rome from Nero to Diocletian. Pergamos was the church that witnessed Rome change its position about those who followed Christ and merge Christianity with the practices of Roman religion. Thyatira was Jezebel's church, where the Roman system was so enticing that people of faith were being lured away from what Christ taught and were openly engaging in paganism. Now we come to the church in

Sardis. Historically, it stands for the time of the Reformation, when Christianity was given a new surge of life but then quickly slipped back into dead formalism and complacency.

In the same manner that the parade of nations in Daniel's interpretation gives an accurate account of what would transpire in world history, the character of conduct in these churches depicts what has happened in church history. With the same amount of accuracy, you can see the progress that is building toward the ultimate conclusion. In the case of Nebuchadnezzar's statue, it was the rock that fell from heaven. This is the establishment of the final kingdom that comes from heaven (see Revelation 19:11–16). In the case of the church, it builds to the Rapture, which is described in Revelation 4. That's when the church is taken out of the earth and, quite literally, all hell will break loose on the world we've left. The point is, the people described in this congregation are not going to make the trip. They are those commonly known as the ones "left behind."

Now many have wrongly thought that, even though these people are left behind, they will still be able to refuse the mark of the beast, resist the Antichrist, and earn their salvation, albeit by losing their head and being martyred. But there are a number of challenges with this doctrine. First, once the Rapture occurs, the day of grace is over. The church is gone. The Holy Spirit is no longer on the earth. Second, how is it reasonable that those who refused to live for God when there were other believers on the earth to encourage them will suddenly find the inner strength to stand against the entire world system? Third, you can't earn salvation. It is a gift that is received by faith. Even if some lost their head, if they didn't have the faith to declare Christ as Savior when the Holy Spirit prompted them as He dwelled on the earth, is it reasonable to believe they would have the faith at that moment in time? The Bible once again puts it plainly and in a manner that all can understand. *Today* "is the day of salvation" (2 Corinthians 6:2).

A TRAGIC COLLAPSE OF BELIEF

At the time this letter was written, Sardis was a powerful and prosperous city. This was the hometown of Croesus, a wealthy man from whom the phrase "rich as Croesus" comes. The city was so wealthy in part because it was naturally fortified and secure. On three sides there were high cliffs that could not be breached, and on the fourth side there was such a narrow passage into the city that it only took a small group of soldiers within to easily defend the entire city.

The Spirit of God, however, looked within this rich and powerful place and said to the Christian church there, "You may be physically alive, but you are spiritually dead. You have buildings and resources, and everything looks really good on the outside, but on the inside you are a rotting corpse." Why were they considered dead? Because they had abandoned the fundamental truth of the Word of God.

When they began, they believed and practiced the biblical truth that the just will live by faith. But then they drifted into a form of godliness that contained plenty of ritual but no relationship with God and His Word. They did a number of good things and the town liked them, but they just didn't do God's thing.

The basis for a relationship with God is found in one word: *believe*. In the New Testament, we read this word over and over again:[1]

- "As many as received Him, to them He gave the right to become children of God, to those who *believe* in His name."

- "Whoever *believes* in Him should not perish but have eternal life."
- "*Believe* on the Lord Jesus Christ, and you will be saved."
- "If you can *believe,* all things are possible to him who *believes.*"
- "He who *believes* in Him is not condemned; but he who does not *believe* is condemned already, because he has not *believed* in the name of the only begotten Son of God."

The church of Sardis started out with a belief in God but soon departed from that belief and started to rely on the power of self. It was a wonderful thing to tell people that you went to the church of Sardis. They would automatically believe you to be honest and wholesome, and it was good for business, since the community felt you could be trusted. It would open a lot of doors and was the right place to be on Sunday morning. The Sardis church was a community that was more consumed with its identity and reputation than with being identified with Christ.

Do you know any churches like that in the world today? Places that are no more than religious clubs, not houses of healing for those who are hurting? Places with membership lists that can really get things done down at the bank or at city hall but haven't baptized a new convert since the Carter administration? God could not care less how big your building gets or how much your budget has in it; He wants to know how much of Him is in you! It's not how well you are known; it's how well you are making Him known to others. God told the church of Sardis, "You are dead," because they spent more time building their name than they did calling on His name.

Autopsy of the Church of Sardis

None of the previous churches were called dead. As a matter of fact, all of them were given the promise of things to come. So why was this one dead? Let's consider the options.

Cause of Death Option 1: Wealth

Did the church of Sardis die because it was wealthy? It's easy to look at the situation and say, "It's because they had money. After all, 'money is the root of all evil.'" Actually, that is a misquote. The passage reads, "The *love* of money is a root of all kinds of evil" (1 Timothy 6:10). I must say, I personally know some people who are wealthy who love money too much, and I know some people who are poor who love money too much. No, the church was not dead because it was rich financially. God sees money as a tool to do His work. He doesn't care how much of it you have, but He absolutely cares what you do with it. There's no evidence that the church of Sardis misused its God-given wealth.

Cause of Death Option 2: Attack

If money was not the problem, did the church die because of an outside attack? No, the truth is, no church has ever died because of an outside attack. To the contrary, in almost every case, churches that are filled with the love of God and the Word of God tend to grow greatly in seasons of persecution. This is why Jesus said in the Beatitudes, "Blessed are you when they revile and persecute you, and say all kinds of evil against you falsely for My sake" (Matthew 5:11).

I remember several years ago there was an attorney in the city of

San Antonio who made it her mission to slander and attack Cornerstone Church. She used the media and made false claims in court. She did everything she could to silence the influence of our ministry because she hated what we stood for. I'll be honest, it wasn't fun. There were a lot of intense conversations going on in the congregation about it.

One evening, after a church service, an elder asked to see my father privately and requested that he do anything he could to make this woman stop attacking the church he loved.

My dad smiled and said, "Why would I do that? She has done more for the spiritual growth of this church than I could have done in years. Our prayer meetings are filling up with people asking God to defend us. Folks who haven't read the Bible in a long time are searching the Scriptures for answers to her attacks. The services are full with people who want to come in and see what all the fuss is about!"

My father knew the attorney wasn't hurting the church. The more she came after us, the better we were doing.

No, Sardis wasn't dying because it was under attack.

Cause of Death Option 3: Spiritual Hunger

Here we come to the true cause of the church's death in Sardis. The church was dying because of the lack of spiritual hunger in its individual members, which led to their spiritual starvation.

No matter how large or small a church is, it lives or dies on the spiritual appetites of those in the pews. "Blessed are those who hunger and thirst for righteousness, for they shall be filled" (Matthew 5:6). No hunger, no growth. No growth, no life. It's that simple.

The church of Sardis was dead and didn't even know it. They were going through the motions and getting nothing out of it. Why? Because the Word of God, His Holy Spirit, and the gospel of His Son were not there.

Signs of Church Life

We need to take the case of Sardis to heart, because what happened in that congregation in Roman-era Asia can happen in any church today. In fact, there are churches all over the world that are open every Sunday with dead men preaching in the pulpit, lifeless souls sitting in the pews, and no desire to change because the people feel like they have no need to. "I know your works," Christ would say to them. "You are dead!"

We not only need to avoid that kind of spiritual death, but we also need to pursue the most vital life in Christ we can. What I have learned in my years of church ministry is that there are at least a couple of signs of life you should consider when you think about our churches.

First, living things are reproductive and replicate themselves. This is true in every natural relationship, whether plant or animal. It is also true in the God-ordained institution of marriage and in churches. Churches should reproduce themselves by winning other people to Christ. They should reproduce redeemed lives by sharing with others the life-changing power of the gospel.

Second, living things crave. I have four children and thank God every day for their natural craving for food. When we sit around our table at home and have a family dinner, it is a wonderful blessing to see them enjoying their meal, because every bite they put in their mouths is a sure sign of life. It means they are growing and need the food to sustain their strength. If one of them comes to the table and isn't interested in eating, then it tells my wife and me that this child isn't feeling well and needs help in order to regain his or her desire for food.

A lot of anemic souls are sitting in churches where there are one of two possibilities taking place: either there is no living bread being served or they have no desire to eat it. Either way, the outcome is the same. They have no strength to grow, and in their weakened condition, they are easily overcome by anything and everything that can be a danger to their soul.

APPEARING LIKE A THIEF

The church in Sardis had received the Word. "Remember therefore," Christ told them, "how you have received and heard; hold fast and repent" (Revelation 3:3). They heard the truth; they just didn't apply it. Jesus said, "Blessed are those who hear the word of God and keep it!" (Luke 11:28). It's not just what you hear; it's what you do with it.

Listen to the next warning: "I will come upon you as a thief, and you will not know what hour I will come upon you" (Revelation 3:3). The reason that the church of Sardis would not know the hour of His coming is because they simply were not looking for Him. That phrase "as a thief" is a direct reference to the Rapture, when believers will be caught up to meet the Lord in the air in the twinkling of an eye.

Rapture means "caught up." The reason I am explaining the meaning is because there are those who want to argue that, since the word *rapture* is not found in Scripture, then the concept must not be true, but this is exactly what's described in 1 Thessalonians 4:17: "We who are alive and remain shall be caught up together . . . in the clouds to meet the Lord in the air." Earlier in this book, I described the plague the prophet Zechariah saw. The term *atomic bomb* is not found in Scripture, but when you read his description and think about what an atomic weapon can do, you know exactly what Zechariah was talking about.

All of the revelations from Daniel, Zechariah, and Ezekiel to Jesus speaking in the book of Revelation give vivid descriptions of what will take place on earth just before the Rapture and the return of Christ. The reason the church members in Sardis didn't know about the signs is because they were not watching for them. They were ignoring the Scriptures and going on about their lives as if there were no promise of Jesus's soon appearing. It was dangerous behavior then, and it is even more dangerous now. The Bible says, "To those who eagerly wait for Him He will appear a second time" (Hebrews 9:28).

LIFE AMID DEATH

The latter part of the letter to the dead church says this: "You have a few names even in Sardis who have not defiled their garments; and they shall walk with Me in white, for they are worthy" (Revelation 3:4).

If you're like me, you look back at the Reformation and other times in history when people have renewed their commitment to the truth that the just will live by faith, and you say, "Yes!" But we need to remember that simply having the right theology is not enough. People who voice their agreement with proper doctrine can be spiritually dead if they aren't trusting in and following Jesus by the power of the Spirit. And sometimes there are whole churches and even groups of churches filled with people who think they are alive but in reality are dead.

Thankfully, in situations like that, there are usually at least some who do not defile their garments. Let me tell you the story of one person in history who strongly resisted the defiling qualities of his community.

The fifteenth-century preacher named Savonarola of Florence tried to turn the people of his day back from their worldly ways. He would stand before a crowd of people and announce, "Thus saith the Lord."[2]

But because the leaders of the church in Rome viewed his utterance as heresy, he was condemned to be hanged and burned. At his execution the religious leaders declared that Savonarola was to be eternally separated from "the Church militant and the Church triumphant." This was a standard statement at all executions for heresy and was given as a last rite before execution. Savonarola replied, "Not from the Church triumphant. That is not thine to do."[3] Savonarola did not defile his garments. He stayed faithful unto death. He is walking with his Savior today, just as he was promised in John's revelations written centuries before.

We, too, can go to be with the Savior when He comes for us. For as He said, "He who overcomes shall be clothed in white garments, and I will not blot out his name from the Book of Life; but I will confess his name before My Father and before His angels" (Revelation 3:5).

19

PHILADELPHIA: FACING AN OPEN DOOR

See, I have set before you an open door, and no one can shut it.

—Revelation 3:8

This letter, from beginning to end, is the most tenderly written of all the letters to the churches in Asia. There is not a single word of rebuke, but instead there are words of encouragement and blessing throughout.

Like the church in Smyrna, this church had faced opposition from the local Jewish community. Following Jesus had not been easy for them. They may have been feeling battered. They may have even begun to wonder if their detractors were right and they really were not accepted by God. What was their future going to be like?

Jesus said their future was going to be just fine.

In this letter Jesus is described as "He who has the key of David" and "He who opens and no one shuts, and shuts and no one opens" (Revelation 3:7). When you have keys, you have authority. When Christ said He had the keys to death, hell, and the grave, He was telling His followers, "I have authority over them." He is the one who has opened those doors and no one can shut them.

So when Jesus told the church at Philadelphia that He was setting an open door before them, they could be sure it was the truth. Their human and demonic enemies could do nothing to prevent them from going through this door.

As I stated earlier in this book, even though the events of the apocalypse can seem scary, we can have great confidence because God is in control and is working out all things for the good of those who love His Son. We have an open door before us too.

ENTER HERE

To give you a quick preview, in the next chapter we're going to see that in Laodicea Jesus was knocking at a shut door. But here, to the Philadelphians, He is holding open a door that no one could shut. What, specifically, was the open door that Jesus set before the church of Philadelphia?

For one thing, it was probably an open door to serve and glorify God. Even more so, it was probably an open door to enter the presence of God.

Door of Opportunity

The Lord uses His faithful followers. He gives them opportunities to tell others about Him, to help the needy, and to provide an example of godly living. The followers of Christ in Philadelphia had already done much to serve their Savior, and they were going to be able to do more.

But open doors not only speak of opportunity; they also bring challenges. There is no reward worth having if it does not bring with it the risk of failure. There is no success without struggle, but struggle is where strength comes from, and strength is how you succeed. The message is clear. God will open doors for you, but you will have to fight the battles that await you on the other side.

Look at this from a biblical standpoint. The hand of God opened a door for the children of Israel to leave Egypt and inhabit the Promised Land, but they had to fight the giants that were in that land. Was it theirs? Yes! Were the giants real? Absolutely! What was required to get them to leave? Struggle! But only in the struggle did they gain the strength to possess what God had promised them.

In Colossians 4:3, Paul asks his friends to pray that a door might be opened for him to share the hidden truth of Christ, about which he said—listen to this—"for which I am also in chains." He was already in prison for preaching, and he was asking God to open a door for him to preach some more. That is the kind of spirit that was found in Philadelphia. When a door was opened, they rejoiced for the new opportunity and didn't run at the first sign of struggle that came with it.

Door of Heaven

In addition to opportunities in this life, the open door also implied entrance into heaven for the Christians of Philadelphia. The Jewish leaders who were making life hard for these believers may have been telling them that they could never be allowed into the kingdom of the Messiah as long as they were disciples of Jesus of Nazareth. But Jesus Himself told them that they belonged to Him and would live with Him forever.

Notice this. The first thing John the Revelator saw after receiving the seven messages to the churches was "a door standing open in heaven" (Revelation 4:1). We'll look again at this door in the final chapter. But what we need to note now is that John was invited to come up to heaven through the door and there receive visions of what would take place after the Rapture. And this door to heaven was likewise open to the faithful believers in Philadelphia.

This same door is open to all who die holding to the faith of Jesus, all who are trusting in the Savior when He returns for them. It's the entranceway to the presence of God.

ADDING OUR NATURAL TO GOD'S SUPER

Jesus commended this church, as He did most of the churches. In this case, His praise is rather peculiar: "I know your works. . . . You have a little strength" (Revelation 3:8).

At first glance you might see this as some type of insult. But it really is a compliment. Christ was saying, "You don't depend on your ability; you lean on Mine. You don't think you can do it on your own all the time; you know that apart from Me you can do nothing." Remember, it is "not by might nor by power, but by [His] Spirit" that great things are accomplished (Zechariah 4:6).

Another point to note is that the word "strength" is not the kind that describes what you gain in muscle mass. The Greek word is *dunamos,* from which we get the word *dynamite.* It's explosive strength.

When you apply your limited natural strength to God's unlimited supernatural strength, you obtain a massive amount of power with little effort of your own. One of the greatest challenges in life is allowing God to use you in a moment of weakness. When you feel like you simply cannot continue, He pours out upon you His grace in ways you never imagined.

The Philadelphia church was not a large church, and they may not have had much by the standards of man, but they were a powerful church because, rather than be full of themselves, they were full of God. In God's power they had kept God's Word and had refused to deny His name, despite facing satanically inspired opposition.

Their example gives us a chance to consider so many things that we see going right. Look at the number of organizations today that are reaching the world and influencing millions for Christ. Their social media feeds show stadiums, auditoriums, and theaters filled with people gathered to worship Christ. The people behind these ministries may not look like the deacon board that posed for the church bulletin thirty years ago, but they are just as passionate, hungry, and thirsty for God as anyone has ever been.

Furthermore, it seems like nothing can stop them. Many are citizens of nations that at one time were considered closed to the gospel, and yet today they are seeing souls won to Christ because they are exposing lives to the genuine love of God. It is as if God Himself is holding a door open for them that no one can close. You could criticize their approach, but wouldn't it be better to celebrate their success? After all, we're all on Christ's team, right? In the world where we live, we should be walking through the open door of grace, not trying to close it or attacking those who are accessing it.

THREE PROMISES

God was aware of the Philadelphia Christians' service, and due to their faithful perseverance, He gave them three promises.

Enemies Bowing at Their Feet

The first promise was that God Himself was going to make their enemies bow at their feet. Those who planned ways to bring them down were going to see their plans fail. These enemies were going to kneel and see in their humiliation the humble congregation exalted, because the Lord resists the proud but gives grace to the humble (see James 4:6).

Kept from Trials

The second promised reward was that they were going to be kept from the trials that will come upon the whole world. This promise, while it was relevant to the protection that God was going to give this church in the first century, also clearly alludes to the Rapture. God has always planned to take His faithful church from the earth before the judgment of the Tribulation begins. Of course, there are those who want to argue with this interpretation, and they are entitled to do so, but I am personally looking forward to leaving before twenty-one forms of judgment are poured out on the earth. Stay if you wish, but I'd rather be raptured.

Now, notice why the trial will come: "to test those who dwell on the earth" (Revelation 3:10). The word translated "test" means "tempt." What will the people on earth after the Rapture be tempted to do? They will be tempted to take the mark of the beast. As we saw in the economics section of this book, during the Tribulation, the only way you will be able to buy, sell, or trade will be to receive this mark. Those who do take it will condemn their souls to an eternity in hell.

In plain language, the bad news is that hard times are coming. The good news is, if you and I are believers, we're going to be gone before it starts!

Soon to See Jesus

The third promise is "I am coming quickly!" (Revelation 3:11). To those who are not ready to meet Him, this is a word of warning. To those who are ready and waiting, they are welcome words to hear.

Ways to Lose Your Crown

As He drew the message to a close, Christ did give the church of Philadelphia a word of warning—they were not to let anyone take their crown (see Revelation 3:11). This is a reference to their position with God being at potential risk.

Some find this hard to accept. They wonder, *Is it really possible to lose your salvation and thus lose your heavenly reward?* This question may be understandable, but if it were not possible for someone to take your crown, why would this verse be in the Bible? Christ had already implied to the church in Sardis that it was possible they would have their name blotted out of the Book of Life (see Revelation 3:5). Here we see another way to fall short of our eternal reward, by allowing another to take our crown. We don't want to believe it, but it's true.

There are at least four ways you can lose your crown.

Discouragement

During times of struggle, people can become so discouraged that they simply want to quit. The feeling doesn't make you a failure; it makes you a human. Elijah wanted to quit. He told God, "Take my life" (1 Kings 19:4). Job wanted to quit. He complained, "Why did I not die at birth?" (Job 3:11).

There are many ways to encounter discouragement, but whenever you do, don't let it take your crown. Don't quit! Put one foot in front of the other and walk through the issue to the promise that awaits you.

Success

Many people allow success to ruin them just as quickly as discouragement ruins others. Success will breed complacency if you see no need to continue to work and toil since you have all that you think you need. Remember, God will open the door, but you must face what's on the other side. A great many people get so busy being successful that they do not have time for God. They fail to reach their full spiritual potential because they are too content with a little bit of success. As long as God keeps opening doors, walk through them!

Resentment

Resentment shows no favoritism; bitterness can come on us all. We feel we've been wronged, and the old wound we have ignored still hurts too much to deal with, so eventually bitterness takes over our soul. Remember, it is not what happens *to you*; it's what happens *in you* that determines whether or not resentment will consume you and draw you away from the Lord.

Idolatry

As we've seen in the previous several letters, God does not turn a blind eye to anything that takes His place in your life. The reason that He holds us responsible for the sin of idolatry is because we are the ones who willfully choose to either worship the one true God or another, and no one can serve two masters.

IN THE PRESENCE OF GOD . . . FOREVER!

The letter nears its end by saying, "He who overcomes, I will make him a pillar in the temple of My God, and he shall go out no more" (Revelation 3:12). Here is a beautiful assurance, drawing deeply from Old Testament–era worship. King David wrote, "A day in Your courts is better than a thousand" (Psalm 84:10). Here the promise is for those who keep their crown and are faithful to the end—they will never have to leave God's presence again.

The church of Philadelphia was a faithful church, and God opened many doors for them to be used for His purpose. That kind of church exists on the earth today in every sanctuary where the Word of God is preached, the work of His kingdom is being done, and Christ is exalted. The promise is real: the day is coming soon when we will be caught up to meet Him in the air.

20

LAODICEA: TEPID FAITH BEFORE THE APOCALYPSE

I know your works, that you are neither cold nor hot.
I could wish you were cold or hot. So then, because you are lukewarm,
and neither cold nor hot, I will vomit you out of My mouth.

—Revelation 3:15–16

In this last of the seven letters, the church in the town of Laodicea is called "lukewarm," meaning neither hot with a burning passion for God nor cold, totally closed off to God. Christ hates this middle state. Why? Because these are the people who are the hardest to reach. They feel like they have done enough, been good enough, and performed well enough, so they see no need for further commitment. This type of person is comfortable when the sermon doesn't confront sin nor call for a change. They constantly speak about being nonjudgmental and allowing everyone to find their own way. They are the people who watch the world around them walk right into the fires of hell and don't feel compelled in any way to warn them about the path they are on. They identify themselves as believers but do not behave like believers because they don't want to be considered fanatics.

These are the people Paul warned Timothy about. "Lovers of themselves, . . . having a form of godliness but denying its power" (2 Timothy 3:2, 5). Their lukewarm behavior is the cause of their ineffectiveness because they have no sense of conviction regarding the faith they claim to possess.

This attitude is the exact opposite of what caused the early church to grow. As we have seen, the most faithful among the first-century believers "did not love their lives to the death" (Revelation 12:11). But the lukewarm church stays home when it rains. The early church did all they could to tell anyone who would listen about the Christ whom they had received. The lukewarm church would prefer to believe that everyone is already saved, because that's easier than sharing your faith with your neighbors across the street. The Laodicean church had no passion for God, and Christ took offense to it.

Here is what we need to recognize. This last letter represents the final age of church history—our time period. *We* are the Laodicean church! As a whole, Christianity is lukewarm today, and sadly this prevents us from providing the strong witness to salvation in Christ that is more critical than ever, now that we stand so close to the second coming. But this doesn't mean you and I and other individual believers and churches can't go against the general trend. We can be hot spots within a mostly lukewarm church. Before the Rapture comes and we lose our chance to witness to others, shouldn't we be fanning the flames of our love for God, standing boldly for His values and truth, and speaking lovingly of His grace to every person we can?

Shouldn't we live out a personal passion for the Lord?

THE POWER OF PASSION

Everything you achieve in your life will be the by-product of passion. Every major breakthrough and invention was the result of someone's passion to solve a problem. Every major social reform was birthed by the passion of those who were willing to stand up and speak out for what they believed. Consider the passion of leaders like Abraham Lincoln, who was willing to do whatever was needed to end the social injustice of slavery in America. What was it that drove Dr. Martin Luther King Jr. to proclaim to the world that he had a dream? Passion. Even in the social issues that you may or may not believe in today, those who are advocating for them are full of passion about what they want and why they want it.

The problem with the lukewarm church is that they do not have enough passion to believe they need anything at all. Don't be like them! Without passion, you will never reach your full potential. Winners go all out because, to them, failure is not an option. The lukewarm spectate and critique, while the passionate compete for victory. One is content to exist until life has passed by, and the other is crowned a champion.

If you are a passionate person in a lukewarm world, you are going to be criticized. Who cares? Be passionate anyway! Refuse to bow to the pressure of complacency, and be the absolute best you can be. Just know that your passion is an irritant to those who want to remain comfortable.

SPEWED OUT

The church is supposed to be a reflection of Christ. When the world looks at us, they are supposed to see Him. Romans 8:29 tells us that we are "to be conformed to the image of His Son." So the reason the lukewarm church is going to be spewed (or spit out) in disgust is because they are a misrepresentation of who Christ is and what He does.

When Christ walked this earth, He was intense. He was so full of passion that He would weep for the people He saw suffering as He prayed for them and for the things He knew in prophecy. Jesus would go out of His way to help those who were in need of ministry—the outcasts, the demon possessed, the lost. He was so passionate that the organized religion of His day worked with the pagan government to label Him a rebel and considered Him such a threat that they got Him condemned to die. Not because He never spoke up, not because He didn't turn heads, not because He was popular and politically correct, but because Jesus was so full of passion for His purpose on earth that nothing was going to stop Him.

The consequence for the Laodiceans' being lukewarm was that they would be "spued out" (Revelation 3:16, KJV). But how? This is a word picture that describes what will occur to all lukewarm people during the Rapture of the church. The faithful will be caught up; the lukewarm will be left behind. One group is leaving the earth while the other will remain during the days of judgment that are to come. Christ spews them out because, while they said they were His, they were not. The only hope for this church is found in Revelation 3:19: "As many as I love, I rebuke and chasten. Therefore be zealous and repent."

ASPECTS OF REPENTANCE

Maybe you have been affected by the lukewarm ways of today's church. Maybe you are feeling the conviction of the Holy Spirit in your heart. What can you do about it? The seventh letter shows the way.

Face the Facts

The first step in repentance is to face the facts about being lukewarm. The Laodicean church said, "We are rich and need nothing." That was their opinion, but it obviously was not God's position. Jesus said, "[You] do not know that you are wretched, miserable, poor, blind, and naked" (Revelation 3:17). They had slipped into such self-deception that they were convinced they were the exact opposite of what God saw them as.

They said, "We have need of nothing." God saw them and said, "You need everything."

We must first face the facts about what we truly need, and then we must be willing to change it.

Return to the Word

The second thing that must be done is to use gold to buy white garments so that you may be clothed. This "gold" is not any form of earthly currency. Look closely at what the text specifically says: "I counsel you to buy from Me gold refined in the fire" (Revelation 3:18). This verse directly speaks of the Word of God. The Word is as pure gold that has been refined in the fire seven times, which means the Word is pure—100 percent pure. The Word is the only way to receive the robes of righteousness, which are the white garments that cover the shame and nakedness discussed in the remainder of the verse.

The message to the lukewarm church is to get back to the Word—preaching it, teaching it, applying it, and telling others what it has done in their lives. Without the Word, there is no hope of a change.

Let Christ In

The final remedy for being lukewarm is to let Christ back into the church. He says, "Behold, I stand at the door and knock" (Revelation

3:20). This church, through their passive contentment, had pushed out the presence of Christ. A lot of buildings in the world today have His name over the door and yet lack His presence inside. But even though He detests what the Laodicean church and others like it have done, and even though they have been warned that in days to come He will spew them out, He's still knocking. He still longs for relationship even with those who are not representing Him as they should. Even in a moment of rebuke and correction He lovingly longs to mend what is broken. What a merciful and loving Savior!

OPENING THE DOOR

"If anyone hears My voice . . ." (Revelation 3:20). To me, these words are haunting.

I know many people who tell themselves that if God ever spoke to them, they would know it. The truth is, He speaks to us all the time. Every morning when you see the sun rise, He is telling the world His mercy has once again been renewed. When you feel the wind on your face, He is reminding you that He is the master of the wind. The moon that glows at night is a constant reminder that He is still keeping His covenant. Rainbows remind us that He will never destroy the earth with a flood again. The stars that we cannot count and are still discovering—the Bible tells us that He has numbered all of them and calls them by name.

All around us, He is knocking on the door. Every day He is speaking, "Let Me in!" In all of these things, God is saying, "Allow Me to be the Lord of your life."

If you hear Him, you have to take action. That is opening the door. The Bible is so consistent. We are told that faith without works is dead (see James 2:14–26). If you hear His voice, you will hear it with faith. When you do, you must respond. You have to welcome Him in before He will enter into the situation. There are a great number of people who want the Lord to intervene in their lives. The reason that He has not intervened has nothing to do with whether or not He wants to. Believe me, He wants to so badly that He came and gave His life as a sacrifice so that He could. The problem is, they haven't opened the door. They have yet to say yes to the gentle knock on the door.

For the one who says yes, the Lord then says of him, "I will come in to him and dine with him, and he with Me" (Revelation 3:20). What a beautiful picture of how Christ longs to share everyday life with you!

Dinnertime is a sacred time at my house. It is the moment when everything I truly care about and live for is in one place together. The outside world is on the other side of the door, and my family gets to share the wins and losses of the day, encourage each other, and feel the healing power of love. This is exactly what Christ uses as the picture of what He will do for those who open the door. He will dine with you. He will share every day with you. He will celebrate the successes and mourn the failures, and He will walk you through it all.

Time is indeed short. All of the signs have been fulfilled. All of the final characters have made their appearance on the stage. The last moments of the world as we know it are coming to a sudden and abrupt end, and to those who are not living a life filled with passion for God, He is still knocking and calling, "Let Me in before it's too late."

Will you answer?

WHAT'S NEXT?

*After these things I looked, and behold, a door standing open
in heaven. And the first voice which I heard was like a trumpet
speaking with me, saying, "Come up here, and I will show you
things which must take place after this."*

—Revelation 4:1

The end times encompass much more than what we have focused on
in this book. In particular, I've noticed that people tend to be fixated
by the seven-year period of the Tribulation and Great Tribulation. This
is the time in which the Antichrist will wreak havoc on the nations of
the world and anyone who does not bow before him. The book of Revelation states that it will get so miserable on earth that people will crawl
into the cracks of rocks and beg God to let the rocks fall on them, because they no longer want to live. But rather than find the escape of
death, they will be forced to face hell on earth. Fascinating these seven
years may be . . . but certainly not pleasant to consider.

Now there's nothing wrong with studying the passages of Scripture
that deal with what comes after the Rapture. If the Lord delays long
enough, I may write other books on those topics. But even if it's good to
know about the horrors that will one day occur on earth, if we are

believers in Jesus, we don't have to be anxious about them. We'll be gone before then! The Rapture will soon and suddenly occur, and we will escape the hardships to come. Being ready for this event is what we should be most focused on, and so that's what I've written about in this book.

To be honest, though, I haven't always been as focused on being Rapture-ready as I am today. Even though many times I heard my grandfather, father, and other faithful people talk about going to meet Jesus in the clouds, as a young person I was more interested in experiencing life down here on earth. I spent several nights in my childhood and teen years staring at the ceiling fan and asking God not to come back until I had the chance to get my driver's license. Once I got to experience driving, I picked a new target: graduation from high school. Everyone should have a diploma before they go to glory, right? Then I wanted to experience college, marriage, fatherhood.

Recently, though, I have come to see the appeal of the Rapture happening soon.

The other day, my wife and I were having dinner at home with our children, and I asked each of them to tell me about their day—you know, "How are your friends? Your teachers? Your coaches?" As the focus of the conversation turned to my eleven-year-old, Hannah, I asked her about a boy she has known since nursery days, and rather than respond, she *blushed!* Suddenly, I knew why my father and every other preacher I knew were so excited for the Rapture. They had no way of stopping their precious little children from becoming teenagers. For the first time in my life, I changed my prayer from "Lord, wait until I can . . ." to "Lord, get here before she goes on her first date!"

Kidding aside, there isn't one thing in our lives that will either speed up or slow down the appointed time of the Rapture, the Tribulation, or the millennial reign and new earth that will follow. This entire book has been about gathering facts of history, the prophecies of the Bible, and the current events of the world around us to prepare us for what is going to happen next, not giving you a play-by-play of what comes after. I'd rather help you be prepared for the Rapture than provide a vivid description of what those who rejected Jesus Christ in this life are going to have to face.

In this final chapter, I will present what's going to happen next, but I want to make sure that you understand it's eternally important to be aware and prepared, not doubting and debating, when the moment comes.

LET'S REVIEW

When discussions turn to the Rapture, the first thing people typically ask is, "How can you be so sure it's coming soon?" Now *you* know the reasons why.

We began by looking at what Daniel interpreted for Nebuchadnezzar, which clearly depicted every global power from the kingdom of Babylon to Rome and its remnants. We are in the period of the iron and clay in the ankles and feet of the statue. We are watching the world form into ten nations or nation groups. Yes, there are certainly more than that currently, but in a world as militarily powerful and economically unstable as the one where we live, things can change quickly.

Then we considered the words of Jesus Christ, primarily found in Matthew 24, and how vividly they described what would occur in Jerusalem and to the Jewish people from AD 70 to the present. It has all happened. The temple was destroyed to the point that not one stone was left on top of the other. The Jewish people were persecuted and scattered all over the world. But then suddenly—in a day—a nation was born in 1948, and the day of the Gentiles ended in 1967 when Jerusalem was returned to the control of the nation of Israel.

History and the Bible point to the Rapture and so does the economy. The world is racing toward the moment when it will willingly accept someone who will be able to make the economy work again. The enslavement of one nation to another through debt in an interconnected global economy, along with climate change activism that promotes "green energy" regardless of financial realities, will cause the world to seek an economic savior. What people won't realize at first is that this "savior" is evil, beastlike, and the opposite of Christ.

Next, we took an honest look at our modern culture. As the Bible warns, wickedness is becoming widespread and blandly accepted in our day as an attitude of selfishness reigns. Meanwhile, our technology and our weapons of mass destruction give us the ability to cause unbelievable destruction. All of this, too, shows that we are ready for the final conflicts to come upon us.

Then, in the most recent series of chapters, we have seen the story of the apocalypse from the perspective of the church. In the seven letters, Christ describes not only the attitudes and character of today's church but also its history from the day of its birth at Pentecost to the present. All along, the church has had its ups and downs. It's never been perfect. We can take warnings from every church age. But in particular we need to recognize that we live in an age of lukewarm Christianity—passionless Christianity, powerless Christianity, a Christianity that's doing little to stand in the way of the progress of evil. And we need to make sure that we are acting as exceptions to the rule, living with a burning zeal for God just as the Lord Jesus Christ did.

The Bible repeatedly proves it is an accurate and powerful source for prophecy as it pertains to all who are on the earth. No matter if they are believers in Christ, committed to the teachings of the Torah, or simply without faith and living in the world without a clue of what's going on, the Word of God has not missed one detail. It is all in writing, and it can all be trusted down to the last letter.

Our job is to be looking up, because Jesus will be coming for us.

When the Trumpet Sounds

The apostle Paul vividly described the Rapture and what will happen in our own generation of believers. To the Corinthians, he said:

> Behold, I tell you a mystery: We shall not all sleep, but we shall all be changed—in a moment, in the twinkling of an eye, at the last trumpet. (1 Corinthians 15:51–52)

To the Thessalonians, he wrote:

> We who are alive and remain until the coming of the Lord will by no means precede those who are asleep. For the Lord Himself will descend from heaven with a shout, with the voice of an archangel, and with the trumpet of God. And the dead in Christ will rise first. Then we who are alive and remain shall be caught up together with them in the clouds to meet the Lord in the air. And thus we shall always be with the Lord. (1 Thessalonians 4:15–17)

The twinkling of an eye takes only fractions of a second to occur, so Paul was picturing how quickly we will be caught up into heaven. And what about after that?

The moments after the Rapture are described in Revelation 4:1–4. Note these key points:

- The chapter begins with "After these things . . ." (verse 1). So this is after the last letter is written to the last church of the last age. That's when John saw a door open to heaven. When he went through it, he began to describe what he saw.

- John observed, "On the thrones I saw twenty-four elders" (verse 4). Who were these elders? They were twelve men chosen from the Old Testament time and twelve from the New Testament time. It is a picture of the complete church (the church triumphant) in heaven. What is the church doing? They are seated. Why? Because the Bible states, "[God] made us sit together in the heavenly places in Christ Jesus" (Ephesians 2:6).

- The elders were "clothed in white robes" (Revelation 4:4). The color white symbolizes righteousness for those who have been forgiven of sin. They are also wearing the crowns that Christ promised to those who overcome. "Be faithful until death," He said, "and I will give you the crown of life" (Revelation 2:10).

John, as he entered through the door to heaven, saw the whole church, those who have died in the faith before us and all who believe now, in heaven, seated at the throne of God. After the Rapture, we will dwell in glory with God until the time when Christ takes us with Him to live in the renewed earth.

After the Rapture, there's no more pain for us. No more fear. No more death, sickness, or hardship. Praise be to God! Every one of us *should* be excited about the Rapture, no matter what our age or what else we may be looking forward to experiencing here on earth.

WAR IN THE LATTER TIMES

After we are gone, the Tribulation will begin for those who are left behind. All hell will literally break loose. These are the days of which Jesus told His disciples, "Unless those days were shortened, no flesh would be saved" (Matthew 24:22). And right now—today—the world is poised for the violence that will break out, with Israel in the center of the crosshairs.

The world is currently racing toward an all-out war in the Middle East. Ezekiel 38 tells of a coalition led by Gog, from the land of Magog, who is the prince of Rosh. In order to understand all of the names, you have to study the descendants of the sons of Noah in Genesis 10, particularly Ham and Japheth. In history, the sons of Ham settled in North Africa, parts of the Middle East, and around the Mediterranean in Turkey and southern Europe. Japheth's descendants settled in Saudi Arabia, Indochina, the Far East, and the "north country," which is present-day Russia (Jeremiah 6:22; 50:9). Among the sons of Japheth was Magog. He settled in the land the prophet Ezekiel calls Magog, and he named the rulers of that land Gog. The capital city was called Rosh, which gave its name to today's Russia.

Ezekiel tells how God draws Gog, the ruler, and Magog, the land, into a battle that involves several other nations. Among them are Persia (present-day Iran); Ethiopia, which represents several modern African nations; and Libya, which is still known by the same name today. Included in this mix are Gomer, who is also a son of Japheth who settled in modern-day Germany; Togarmah, which is more of the former Soviet Union; and "many peoples with you" (Ezekiel 38:9, 15).

In verse 8, Ezekiel uses the phrase "in the latter years." That is a prophetic phrase describing a time when Christ has poured out His

Spirit on all flesh, as prophesied by Joel and fulfilled on the day of Pentecost (see Joel 2:28–29; Acts 2:1–4). So when Ezekiel said these things, it was not an action that was going to take place in his time, but rather it was destined for the *latter years* that I just described.

He then continued, "You will come into the land of those brought back from the sword and gathered from many people on the mountains of Israel" (Ezekiel 38:8). Who were the people who were gathered? They were the dispersed Jews who were spread all over the world due to persecution that occurred century after century. What brought them back to the land of Israel? The sword of persecution unleashed by Hitler and the Holocaust. With so many families decimated, the Jewish people came from all over the world to Israel, just as Ezekiel described in verse 8, and he even recounted how the land had been desolate for a long time.

The Holy Land was once a relatively lush place, then it became more desolate, and now it is in the process of being restored to a greener state. The historical reason for the period of barrenness in the land is that the Ottoman Empire in the late 1800s decided to tax the Jews who were then living in Palestine for every tree that grew on their property. Rather than pay the exorbitant tax, they cut the trees down. Without trees to hold the soil in the rainy season, the ground became bare and the land was desolate. But the land that Gog and Magog and their coalition of armies are coming against is not desolate. Those who would gather there will cause the once-desolate land of Israel to thrive again. Here is another fulfillment of prophecy in which the Bible states, "The desert shall rejoice and blossom as the rose" (Isaiah 35:1). Modern Israel is in the process of irrigating, planting, and making the land bloom again.

It is important to point this out so that you are aware of when this war takes place:

1. Not in the time of Ezekiel, but in the "latter years" after the church is born
2. After those who were scattered have been gathered back to the land returned to Jewish control in 1948
3. Not when the land is desolate, but when it is flourishing again, namely in present-day Israel
4. And finally, when the scattered Jews have been "brought out of the nations" and now "dwell safely" in Israel (Ezekiel 38:8)

The time and description that Ezekiel gives is of the modern State of Israel, not the ancient one of the Bible.

The Stage Is Now Set

So what is happening in the world today that is making all of this relevant? A lot.

The Russia-Iran Alliance

Right now, Russia is in the Middle East helping Iran as much as it can. And meanwhile the United States has given Iran a path to create and possess nuclear weapons. On his trip to Hiroshima, President Barack Obama spoke of his hope for a world without nuclear weapons, and yet our State Department, under the leadership of John Kerry, has given Iran—a known global supporter of terrorism and enemy of Israel and the United States—a chance to have those weapons.[1] It is diplomatic insanity, to say the least! Nevertheless, it means that what the prophet Ezekiel was talking about is starting to unfold every night as you watch the evening news and hear national security experts talk about the dangers of Iran and ask the question, "What are we going to do about

Russia?" The answer to their question? We are not going to do one solitary thing. We are just going to sit back and watch what Russia does.

Ezekiel continues, "You will ascend, coming like a storm, covering the land like a cloud, you and all your troops. . . . On that day it shall come to pass that thoughts will arise in your mind, and you will make an evil plan" (Ezekiel 38:9–10).

The enemies of Israel will come for two reasons. First, Russia wants to be known as the world's superpower, and the weakness that the United States and the West have shown is only encouraging them more. Second, the Persians (modern-day Iran) are coming because they have hated Israel since the days of Haman and Mordecai, recorded in the book of Esther. Iran is currently under the leadership of a radical ayatollah who believes that he practices the true Islam and that it is the will of Allah to annihilate the Jewish people, wiping Israel from the face of the earth. The other members of the coalition may have different and various political reasons for why they are willing to join the fight, but the root cause of the battle is old-fashioned anti-Semitism.

America's Greed

The only possible hindrance to this massive military effort is from Tarshish "and all their young lions" (Ezekiel 38:13). This group will ask a stupid question: "Have you come to take plunder? Have you gathered your army to take booty, to carry away silver and gold?" Really?

Tarshish is modern-day Gibraltar, a small region at the tip of the Iberian peninsula. Gibraltar is officially a British Overseas Territory. What is displayed on the Royal Arms of England? Three lions.

Now America, by historical standards, is considered a new nation, and it got its start as a British colony, so the young lion in this prophetic verse could represent the United States. And, according to the text, all we will do is look at what the coalition of Israel's enemies are doing and ask, "Are you here to take home some treasure?" If that doesn't sound like the Obama administration's diplomatic approach to solving the world's problems, I don't know what does.

Israel's Sole Defender

Ezekiel 38 continues in verse 16: "You will come up against My people Israel." That is an important phrase because there are a lot of people who falsely teach that God is through with Israel. Not according to His own words in this verse. God calls them "My people." He goes on to say, "I will bring you against My land." Again, this is very important because a popular opinion today is that the land doesn't belong to Israel. Well, in a way that is correct, because according to Ezekiel 38:16, it belongs to God ("My land"). But since it belongs to Him, He can give it to whomever He wants. And God gave the land grant to Abraham, Isaac, and Jacob. So you can protest all you want about who it belongs to, but as far as God is concerned, it is still their land and Israel is still His people.

Read why God was going to allow this: "so that the nations may know Me, when I am hallowed in you, O Gog, before their eyes." God is once again setting the stage to show the world who He is through His awesome power and might.

In the balance of the chapter, Ezekiel tells how no other nation will come to the aid of Israel, but God in heaven is going to defend them. He will use the forces of nature to crush this military machine and so decimate them. At the end of the chapter, God tells Gog, "Thus I will magnify Myself and sanctify Myself, and I will be known in the eyes of many nations. Then they shall know that I am the LORD" (verse 23).

American Passivity, the Certainty of War, and the Emergence of the Antichrist

This scenario is much closer to becoming a news alert than you might imagine. Just consider how everything that is happening in the world today is leading right to this very moment in time that you have just read about. In my country, many of us would like to believe that America's military would come to Israel's aid in a crisis. Under the past administration, however, our nation's military was scaled down to pre–World War II levels.[2] The last time we were in this position, Japan attacked us because they didn't believe we had the ability to respond. We did respond effectively in World War II. This time, however, the opinion will be correct, because not only will we not have the ability to respond in a rapidly developing war, but we won't possess the desire either.

Some might look to a new leader for hope in this area. As I write this, Donald Trump has recently been elected to serve as the forty-fifth president of the United States. He has made many sweeping promises and has created quite a stir with his approach to addressing the direction of the United States and its role in the world. While many of those aspirations may be laudable, the truth is, election day is when the work begins, not when it ends. Many are going to continue to use their power and conniving to weaken American support for Israel. There's no guarantee that a new leader, even if well intentioned in this area, can reverse the ongoing trend for Israel to have to go it alone against her enemies.

So why should this matter? Because this is no small conflict. When God gets done defending Israel, the world is going to be in total chaos. Russia, Iran, Germany, Turkey, Libya, and several other nations are going to be militarily destroyed. The impact will have huge economic ramifications. These countries will go into an economic free fall, taking the global market with them. This scenario is tailor-made for the final satanic leader to emerge and bring to the world what it wants: stability and peace. Then add to this another feature. Sometime, in close proximity to this battle, either before or after, millions of believers in Jesus Christ will suddenly vanish off the face of the earth.

READY OR NOT

It's not a matter of *if* all this happens; it is only a matter of *when*. God has revealed it in His apocalypse—His unveiling. And it is absolutely true.

When the Rapture does occur, will you be ready? Not with a bunker full of bottled water and food rations, but will your soul be in the right place? Will you have given your heart and life to the One who promised that if you would believe in Him you would have everlasting life? The only way to prepare for the events that I have shared in this book is to surrender your life to Christ and to do it today, because in the world where we are living, tomorrow may be too late.

ACKNOWLEDGMENTS

I t goes without saying that each and every achievement and project completed requires the work of an entire team to achieve success. I would like to thank the dedicated team members who contributed to this book, both from Hagee Ministries and WaterBrook.

To Jo-Ann Coffey, Melissa Krock, and the dedicated staff of our ministry: without your consistent efforts hardly anything could or would get done.

To Duncan Dodds and Big Vision Advisors: your direction has been greatly appreciated in the season of this ministry that we look forward to sharing many more moments to come.

To the team members from WaterBrook and editors Laura Barker and Eric Stanford: every one of you are greatly appreciated and respected for your great work and efforts.

To my wife, Kendal, who manages the most important team that I'm on: my four fabulous children and our home. You are the heartbeat of my world and I can't tell you how much I appreciate your support in all things.

Finally, to my parents. Dad, you taught me the Word and the Word never returns void. Mom, you supported Dad, and without you both I wouldn't be the man that I am today.

NOTES

CHAPTER 3: SIGNS OF THE END OF THE AGE

1. Flavius Josephus, *The Wars of the Jews, or the History of the Destruction of Jerusalem,* book V, chapter 10, paragraph 3, www.sacred-texts.com/jud /josephus/war-5.htm.
2. Bruce, aka Caitlyn, Jenner was named Transgender Champion. "Glamour's Women of the Year 2015: Reese Witherspoon, Victoria Beckham, Misty Copeland, and More Honorees," *Glamour,* October 29, 2015, www .glamour.com/story/woty-2015-winners.
3. Glenn Stanton, "What Is the Actual US Divorce Rate and Risk?" Public Discourse, December 16, 2015, www.thepublicdiscourse. com/2015/12/15983/.
4. Chris Hedges, "What Every Person Should Know About War," *New York Times,* July 6, 2003, www.nytimes.com/2003/07/06/books/chapters /what-every-person-should-know-about-war.html?_r=0.

CHAPTER 4: A CRESCENDO OF HATRED

1. David A. Rausch, *Legacy of Hatred: Why Christians Must Not Forget the Holocaust* (Grand Rapids, MI: Baker, 1990), 27.
2. See Habakkuk 2:4 and Romans 1:17; also see Hebrews 10:38.
3. See Martin Luther's 1523 essay "That Jesus Christ Was Born a Jew." www .ccjr.us/dialogika-resources/primary-texts-from-the-history-of-the -relationship/272-luther-1523.
4. Martin Luther, *The Jews and Their Lies* (1543), Jewish Virtual Library, www.jewishvirtuallibrary.org/jsource/anti-semitism/Luther_on_Jews.html.
5. Léon Poliakov, *From the Time of Christ to the Court Jews,* vol. 1 in *The History of Anti-Semitism,* trans. Richard Howard (1955; repr., Philadelphia: University of Pennsylvania Press, 2003), 220.
6. Michael Qazvini, "Report: Obama Administration Prepares to Smack Israel," Daily Wire, May 9, 2016, www.dailywire.com/news/5564/report -obama-administration-prepares-smack-israel-michael-qazvini#.

CHAPTER 5: THE GREATEST MIRACLE OF OUR TIME

1. See Genesis 15:18; 17:8; 26:3; Numbers 34:2–15; and Joshua 11:16–23; 13:1–23.
2. Quoted in "State of Israel Proclaimed," This Day in History: May 14, History, www.history.com/this-day-in-history/state-of-israel-proclaimed.
3. "President Truman's Decision to Recognize Israel," Jerusalem Center for Public Affairs, post by Amb. Richard Holbrooke, May 1, 2008, http://jcpa .org/article/president-truman%E2%80%99s-decision-to-recognize-israel/.
4. Michael T. Benson, *Harry S. Truman and the Founding of Israel,* (Westport, CT: Greenwood, 1997), 189.
5. Chaim Herzog, *The Arab-Israeli Wars* (New York: Random House, 1982), 149.
6. Quoted in "Miracles in the Six-Day War: Eyewitness Accounts," May 7, 2014, Israel National News, www.israelnationalnews.com/News/News .aspx/122435.

CHAPTER 6: HOW THE FINANCIAL DOMINOES WILL FALL

1. Many translations of Scripture use other words, such as "deceit," in place of "craft" in this verse. When you trace the word back to the Hebrew root, however, it becomes clear that a more accurate translation is "craft," referring to financial wealth and global commerce.
2. Kim Hjelmgaard and Roger Yu, "Four Ways U.K.'s Looming 'Brexit' Vote Is Causing Global Shivers," *USA Today,* May 11, 2016, www.usatoday.com /story/news/world/2016/05/11/four-ways-uks-looming-brexit-vote-causing -global-shivers/84175958/.
3. Nick Gutteridge, "European SUPERSTATE to Be Unveiled: EU Nations 'to Be Morphed into One' post-Brexit," *Express* (UK), June 29, 2016, www .express.co.uk/news/politics/683739/EU-referendum-German-French -European-superstate-Brexit.

CHAPTER 7: ENVIRONMENTAL HOSTAGES

1. Barack Obama, press release, "Remarks by the President on Climate Change," White House, June 25, 2013, www.whitehouse.gov/the-press -office/2013/06/25/remarks-president-climate-change.
2. James Conca, "It's Final—Corn Ethanol Is of No Use," Forbes, April 20, 2014, www.forbes.com/sites/jamesconca/2014/04/20/its-final-corn -ethanol-is-of-no-use/#a16bab12ca26.

3. Conca, "It's Final—Corn Ethanol Is of No Use."

4. "Global Warming, Environment and Energy," section 7 of "Beyond Red Versus Blue: The Political Typology," Pew Research Center, June 26, 2014, www.people-press.org/2014/06/26/section-7-global-warming-environment -and-energy/.

CHAPTER 8: TAKING THE MARK OF THE BEAST

1. Andrew Blake, "Identity Theft Affected 17.6M, Cost $15.4B in 2014: Justice Dept.," *Washington Times,* September 28, 2015, www.washingtontimes .com/news/2015/sep/28/identity-theft-affected-176-million-cost -154-billi/.

2. Bob Sullivan, "9/11 Report Light on ID Theft Issues," NBC News, August 4, 2004, www.nbcnews.com/id/5594385/ns/us_news-security/t/report-light -id-theft-issues/#.V45m5VddHPw.

3. "How to Survive in the West: A Mujahid Guide," 2015, www .investigativeproject.org/documents/misc/863.pdf.

4. Stephen Coggeshall, "Time to Retire Social Security Numbers?" August 14, 2014, CNBC, www.cnbc.com/2014/08/14/time-to-retire-social-security -numbersidentity-theftcommentary.html.

5. Phillip Connor, "U.S. Admits Record Number of Muslim Refugees in 2016," Pew Research Center, October 5, 2016, www.pewresearch.org /fact-tank/2016/10/05/u-s-admits-record-number-of-muslim-refugees -in-2016/.

6. Associated Press, "U.S. to Resettle Australia's Refugees Languishing on Pacific Islands," CBS News, November 13, 2016, www.cbsnews.com/news /us-resettle-australia-refugees-languishing-on-pacific-islands/.

7. Phillip Connor, "Number of Refugees to Europe Surges to Record 1.3 Million in 2015," Pew Research Center, August 2, 2016, www.pewglobal .org/2016/08/02/number-of-refugees-to-europe-surges-to-record -1-3-million-in-2015/.

CHAPTER 10: IT'S ALL ABOUT ME

1. John F. Kennedy, Inaugural Address, January 20, 1961, Washington, DC, John F. Kennedy Presidential Library and Museum, www.jfklibrary.org /Asset-Viewer/BqXIEM9F4024ntFl7SVAjA.aspx.

2. I was present when San Antonio Assistant Chief of Police Anthony Treviño made this statement.

CHAPTER 11: HIGH-DEF APOCALYPSE

1. Steven Goodman, "How Many People Live to 100 Across the Globe?" Centenarian, August 6, 2016, www.thecentenarian.co.uk/how-many-people -live-to-hundred-across-the-globe.html.

2. "Does Population Growth Impact Climate Change?" *Scientific American,* www.scientificamerican.com/article/population-growth-climate-change/.

3. "Post–World War II Baby Boom," Wikipedia, https://en.wikipedia.org/wiki /Post–World_War_II_baby_boom.

4. Steven Ertelt, "58,586,256 Abortions in America Since Roe v. Wade in 1973," Life News, January 14, 2016, www.lifenews.com/2016/01/14 /58586256-abortions-in-america-since-roe-v-wade-in-1973/.

5. "Live Births, Birth Rates, and Fertility Rates, by Race: United States, 1909–2003," Centers for Disease Control, www.cdc.gov/nchs/data/statab /natfinal2003.annvol1_01.pdf.

6. Catherine Rampell, "Bad News for Older Folks: Millennials Are Having Fewer Babies," *Washington Post,* May 4, 2015, www.washingtonpost.com /opinions/among-millennials-theres-a-baby-bust/2015/05/04/c98d5a08 -f295-11e4-84a6-6d7c67c50db0_story.html?utm_term=.3bb7a6485e28.

CHAPTER 12: THE ARSENAL OF THE FINAL CONFLICTS

1. "The Enola Gay," Nuclear Weapon Archive, http://nuclearweaponarchive .org/Usa/EnolaGay/EnolaGay.html.

2. Michelle Hall, CNN Library, "By the Numbers: World War II's Atomic Bombs," Aug. 6, 2013, www.cnn.com/2013/08/06/world/asia/btn -atomic-bombs/.

3. Quoted in Max Fisher, "The Emperor's Speech: 67 Years Ago, Hirohito Transformed Japan Forever," *Atlantic,* August 15, 2012, www.theatlantic .com/international/archive/2012/08/the-emperors-speech-67-years-ago -hirohito-transformed-japan-forever/261166/.

4. Col. Timothy J. Geraghty, *Peacekeepers at War: Beirut 1983—The Marine Commander Tells His Story* (Washington, DC: Potomac Books, 2009), 185.

5. Majid Rafizadeh, "Iran Breaches the Nuclear Deal and UN Resolutions for Third Time," *Huffington Post,* May 15, 2016, www.huffingtonpost.com /majid-rafizadeh/iran-breached-the-nuclear_b_9977768.html.

6. United Nations Security Council, Resolution 1929, June 9, 2010, www.iaea .org/sites/default/files/unsc_res1929-2010.pdf.

7. Resolution 2231 (2015), "Ballistic Missile-Related Transfers and Activities," United Nations Security Council, www.un.org/en/sc/2231/restrictions -ballistic.shtml.

8. Encyclopedia Britannica online, s.v. "Anti-Ballistic Missile Treaty (ABM Treaty)", www.britannica.com/event/Anti-Ballistic-Missile -Treaty#ref940546.

9. Quoted by Larry Haas, in interview by Edward Stourton, *Current Affairs,* BBC, October 19, 2009, http://news.bbc.co.uk/nol/shared/spl/hi /programmes/analysis/transcripts/19_10_09d.txt.

CHAPTER 14: EPHESUS: LETTING GO OF FIRST LOVE

1. *Strong's Concordance,* 2577 *(kamnó).*

CHAPTER 15: SMYRNA: SUFFERING LIKE CHRIST

1. These and other stories of Roman-era Christian martyrs can be found in any edition of *Foxe's Book of Martyrs* by John Foxe.

2. John Foxe, *Foxe's Book of Martyrs* (Nashville: Thomas Nelson, 2000), 15–16.

3. "The Martyrdom of Saints Perpetua and Felicitas," PBS.org. From *The Acts of the Christian Marytrs,* texts and translation by Herbert Musurillo (Oxford: Clarendon Press, 1972), www.pbs.org/wgbh/pages/frontline /shows/religion/maps/primary/perpetua.html.

4. William J. Cadigan, "Christian Persecution Reached Record High in 2015, Report Says," CNN, January 17, 2016, www.cnn.com/2016/01/17/world /christian-persecution-2015/.

5. Christiane Maria Cruz de Souza, "The Spanish Flu Epidemic: A Challenge to Bahian Medicine," The Scientific Electronic Library Online, Brazil, www .scielo.br/scielo.php?script=sci_arttext&pid=S0104-59702008000400004 &lng=en&tlng=en.

6. "Flu Vaccine," eMedicineHealth, www.emedicinehealth.com/flu_vaccine /page2_em.htm.

CHAPTER 16: PERGAMOS: TEMPTED BY COMPROMISE

1. "Roman Paganism: The Religion of Rome," The Illustrated History of the Roman Empire, www.roman-empire.net/religion/religion.html. Also, MaryTruth.com, www.marytruth.com/home/constantine-cover -up-and-sun-worship.

CHAPTER 17: THYATIRA: TOLERATING FALSE TEACHING

1. For Jezebel's story, see 1 Kings 16:31; 18:4; 19:1–2; 21; and 2 Kings 9.
2. The first to describe the Semmerimus-Tammuz religious tradition was Alexander Hislop in *The Two Babylons* (1853).

CHAPTER 18: SARDIS: MORE DEAD THAN ALIVE

1. John 1:12; 3:15; Acts 16:31; Mark 9:23; John 3:18
2. John Lord, "Savonarola," World Spirituality, www.worldspirituality .org/savonarola.html.
3. Philip Schaff, *The Middle Ages, A.D. 1294–1517,* vol. 6, *History of the Christian Church,* www.ccel.org/ccel/schaff/hcc6.iii.x.v.html.

CHAPTER 21: WHAT'S NEXT?

1. "Obama Speech at Hiroshima," YouTube video, posted by VOA Op-Ed, May 27, 2016, www.youtube.com/watch?v=xIotBp0TQEk; and Adam Kredo, "Iran 'Blackmailing' U.S. for Greater Nuke Concessions," Washington Free Beacon, May 24, 2016, http://freebeacon.com/national-security /iran-blackmailing-us/.
2. Jim Tice, "Army Shrinks to Smallest Level Since Before World War II," *Army Times,* May 7, 2016, www.armytimes.com/story/military/careers /army/2016/05/07/army-shrinks-smallest-level-since-before-world-war-ii /83875962/.

ABOUT THE AUTHOR

Matthew Charles Hagee is the sixth generation in the Hagee family to carry the mantle of gospel ministry. He serves as the executive pastor of the twenty-thousand-member Cornerstone Church in San Antonio, Texas, where he partners with his father, founding pastor John Hagee.

Matt's teachings and faith-based talk shows, *The Difference* and *Hagee Hotline,* are telecast throughout the world on radio and television, as well as twenty-four hours a day, seven days a week at GETV.org through John Hagee Ministries. He is fervently committed to preaching all the gospel to all the world and to all generations.

In addition to being a teacher, Matt is an accomplished vocalist and founder of the Dove Award–winning gospel quartet Canton Junction. His love for music led him to cofound Difference Media, a music label with the goal of reaching the lost and spreading God's truth through song.

A graduate of Oral Roberts University School of Business, Matt is the author of *Shaken, Not Shattered* and *Response-Able.*

He and his wife, Kendal, are blessed with four children. As their family and ministry grow, Pastor Matt and Kendal seek to fulfill their God-given mission with the passion and purpose that can only come from the power of family tradition and the anointed call of God on their lives.

For topical and current-event teaching videos by Matt Hagee
related to the content in this book, please visit
Jhm.org/apocalypse